Pithecophilia

by
Robert Louis DeMayo

4/7/21

Available on Amazon, Ingram, KDP,
and other retailers.

Published in print and as an eBook.

Edited by **Nina Rehfeld**
Nina@txture.com

Technical Edits by **J. Judson Wynne, Ph.D.**
jut.wynne@nau.edu

Cover Design by **Andrew Holman**
www.andrewholman.com

Interior Illustrations by **Tom Fish**
tfishart@yahoo.com

Pithecophilia

Rhesus Macaque
(*Macaca mulatta*).

Pithecophilia

(Pi–thuh–koh–Fi–lee–uh)

The love of apes and monkeys - from the Greek *pithekos* (πίθηκος), "ape, monkey," and *philia* (φιλία) - often translated as "brotherly love."

For your convenience,
a glossary is provided in
the back of this book.

Table of Contents

Book Two – *1994 - 2010*

Final Thoughts – *2020*

Building a fort on our land in Maine. David is holding the stake.

for

David John DeMayo

When we were kids, my dad called my brother David and me, "House Apes." It was an apt nickname. We wrestled and fought. We broke things while chasing each other. We screamed like hell at times. And repeatedly, we dared each other to do some really crazy stuff.

David shared my love of adventure, and we enjoyed playing any game that felt like exploration. He was the designated "test pilot" for all our homemade go-carts, and he got to be an astronaut once when we rolled him in a tractor tire down a hill into a lake, bouncing, at times, nearly ten feet high.

On Sunday nights we anxiously awaited our favorite show, *Wild Kingdom*, especially if they had an episode that was set in Africa. We loved all things African. The walls of our bedroom were festooned with movie posters of *King Kong* and *Tarzan*.

And maybe that was the seed of a feeling like I was in some form of human troop—a tribe that seemed to have an extra close tie to primates. A throwback to something wilder. My parents may have encouraged that too. They were both great storytellers—the first two raconteurs in my life—and they enchanted us with adventurous tales when we spent summers camping on our land in northern Maine.

Pithecophilia

David was my younger brother by almost two years, my first subordinate, and later the first to rebel against my authority as a big brother. But that's what being in a tribe is all about.

When he began tinkering with mechanical devices, my dad dubbed him "the Grease Monkey" and later, when he developed a muscular physique, we called him "the Gorilla."

These may all be reasons I thought of him while I wrote this book, but my motivation to dedicate the story to him is because of his nature.

My brother was solidly muscular when we were younger, and he had one of the highest pain tolerances of any kid I knew. If you tried walking through a doorway at the same time as him, you'd end up mangled against the door frame.

But I don't ever recall him bullying or picking on anyone. And if I was in trouble, he was the first in line behind me. We seemed to understand each other so well that we often didn't need words — very much like some of the primate encounters I recount in this novel.

In 1996 David joined me in Zimbabwe for a month. I write about this in Chapter Ten. We camped at Victoria Falls for a few days, and during that time, we were terrorized by a baboon named Shirley.

Out of the two years that I spent traveling Africa, the month traveling with him, and my mom and wife, are the dearest to me. Not only because we got to spend time together, but because we shared so many hours watching animals, immersing ourselves in nature.

Experiences like that only make the tribe stronger.

So, here's to my brother, David, one of the nicest guys I have ever known, and a proud member of my tribe.

David is on the left with the frisbee. Easter Sunday. 1972.

Pithecophilia

Robert Louis DeMayo

Book One

1976 - 1993

My mountain gorilla image. 1976.

Chapter One

The Photograph
(1976)

When I was twelve, I attended a summer school photography class at Attleboro High School in Massachusetts. As far back as I can remember, I had desperately wanted to learn how to photograph the world around me, particularly animals, and this was my big chance.

My teacher—a man I'll call "Mr. Smith"—asked me to stay after class one day while he developed the film the students had submitted for their finals.

I didn't mind hanging around because Mr. Smith had also promised to use the time to make an enlargement of one of his photos for me. It was an image that so gripped me when I stared at it, that all I could do was imagine myself there, taking the picture.

This vivid image, burned into stark white photo paper, felt so real to me that it seemed more like a forgotten memory; the remembrance of a powerful apparition that hovered slightly beyond my consciousness.

So, while Mr. Smith slowly moved the pieces of glossy photo paper from the developer solution to the fixer, I sat back in the red light and waited, fidgeting in a gloomy dimness that was thick with the acrid smell of photographic processing chemicals.

Suddenly the piercing sirens of a fire alarm arose, and Mr. Smith frowned.

Even at twelve, I understood why: This was the third alarm of the week, and the last two had been false alarms that had cost him dearly. The darkroom had no revolving door, so if you opened the door while the film was being developed, the flood of light overexposed it. Twice, this had happened, and Mr. Smith had to request that his students take replacement photographs and resubmit them.

Now, with the prospect of ruining the classes' film yet again, he looked at me and said, "I'm sure this is a false alarm like the others — let's just finish up quickly and get out of here."

Over the next ten minutes, he hung up the class images to dry, then made the enlargement of his own photograph and dropped it into the developer tub.

The entire time the alarm blared shrilly.

I barely heard it as I anxiously leaned over the tub and stared hard at the image while it slowly came into focus.

At first, all I glimpsed was a blob in the middle, but that soon transformed into the rugged shape of a male mountain gorilla. He stood upright, almost impossibly straight, his elbows bent and his massive hands against his chest as if in mid-beat. Dense foliage and vines grew around him, and behind the impressive animal, several majestic volcanoes faded into the distance.

The fire alarm continued to blare, and that sense of warning was fresh in my mind as I stared into the eyes of the gorilla. I wanted to ask Mr. Smith where he'd taken this photograph, but he seemed too edgy to answer any questions as he packed everything up to get out of the lab.

Eventually, he flipped on the lights and led me out.

I followed, holding my photograph, still wet, by the corners.

The lab was in the basement, under the school pool, and when we opened the door to exit the building, we were greeted by bright sunlight and three fire trucks — all with ladders and hoses pointed at the school building.

Apparently, the bleachers in the pool area had somehow caught fire.

Mr. Smith turned white as he realized we'd been developing photographs just beneath the blaze the entire time.

He leaned down to me and whispered, "If you ever tell anyone about this, I'll lose my job."

I gripped my gorilla image tightly and assured him it was our secret.

Johnny Weissmuller as *Tarzan*. MGM 1932.

Chapter Two

Tarzan
(1977)

*T*he next summer, my mother became the coolest person I knew when she met Tarzan! Johnny Weissmuller, who had played the boy raised by apes in a dozen movies in the thirties and forties, to me was the living embodiment of the literary figure created by Edgar Rice Burroughs.

I was in awe as she described her encounter at a diner in New York City. My mother, Patricia, had spent a few days at a beauty convention in the city with her girlfriend, Judy. Now she was alone at a diner, waiting for her bus home.

She had three hours to pass and sat sipping a coffee when she noticed the man perched on a barstool at the counter was Weissmuller.

He sat there alone, hunched forward. He was then seventy-four years old, well past his days of swing on vines in the movies. And he didn't look well, having suffered a stroke the year before.

My mother approached him and introduced herself.

He seemed flattered that someone still recognized him, and his face lit up when my mother boasted that her two sons were huge fans.

He asked her to sit down on the stool by his side. They talked for the next hour, and when he got up to leave, he made sure she told her sons that Tarzan had said "hi."

My brother and I ran around like mini-Tarzans, yodeling at the top of our lungs when she told us this; even though at first, I don't think I believed her. Our mother had an adventurous soul and was always spinning wild yarns about places like Africa and Alaska, and meeting Tarzan seemed so farfetched that maybe this was just another tale.

But then she pulled a napkin from her purse, and scribbled on it, clear as day, was Johnny Weissmuller's signature.

I gingerly took the napkin and ran into my room. I knew just where to put it.

To an outsider, our room may have looked like a shrine dedicated to Africa and apes. I had my gorilla photo taped to the wall, and our Tarzan comic collection stacked under it. I tacked the signature to the bottom corner of the image, in a place of honor. We also had movie posters and flyers from TV shows that we loved: *A Cowboy in Africa*, starring Chuck Connors as Jim Sinclair, and *Daktari* were two of our favorites.

And every Sunday night, we were seated on the living room floor, in front of the television set, anxiously waiting for Mutual of Omaha's *Wild Kingdom* to begin. This educational series focused on the lives of animals, and much of it was filmed in Africa. Famed naturalist and zoologist Marlin Perkins hosted the show, always accompanied by his young, burly assistant, Jim Fowler. I can't begin to say how envious I was of these men who seemed to stumble upon adventure by the minute.

Often when my brother and I played *Wild Kingdom,* we argued over who stayed in the vehicle as the elderly Perkins, and who got to pretend he was Jim Fowler.

As he did in the show, Jim always had a rough day in our games, often fighting off lions and tackling rhinos.

My favorite movie was *Born Free,* starring Virginia McKenna. The film follows a fictionalized version of the naturalist Joy Adamson on her mission to raise a wild lion cub and then set it free.

I believe I drove my dad half-mad by constantly singing Andy Williams' lyrics to the soundtrack.

"Born free, as free as the wind blows. As free as the grass grows. Born free to follow your heart."

What made the far-off jungles and savannas seem even closer was that we lived a half-mile from the Capron Park Zoo in Attleboro, Massachusetts, and at night I often heard the lions roar when feeding time approached.

There were tigers and other big cats too, but the lions were most vocal.

When I was little and my dad got me mad, I would threaten to have one of my lions from up the street eat him. And if I made this threat around feeding time when we could hear them clearly, it seemed a possibility. I had a giant snake at my command, too.

The zoo also had two gibbons, which I had learned were the smallest of the four members of the ape family. One was black, and the other yellow-white, and they were named Chocolate and Vanilla.

They were my favorite animals at the zoo, and I often shared my popcorn with them. There was a sign that warned not to feed the gibbons, but they seemed to like it so much, staring at me pleadingly with their black hands stretched out between the bars, that I was unable to refuse them.

Many times throughout my childhood, I woke in the middle of a hot summer night to hear a lion's deep cough echoing through our neighborhood. I would glance over at my mountain gorilla, staring back through the gloom, and a yearning to get deeper into Africa rose within me. Would I ever trek through the jungle to see a gorilla, or hear a lion's cough from my tent?

That passion was fueled further when my grandfather began handing down his *National Geographic* magazines. Soon my head was filled with international stories of exploration and science. On my gorilla altar, I added the 1970 feature about Dian Fossey's work with mountain gorillas in Zaire, and another with an article on Jane Goodall's field studies with chimpanzees in Tanzania.

I learned about naturalists and conservationists like Carl Akeley and George Schaller, and about Roy Chapman Andrews and his expeditions to Mongolia to find fossils.

And I followed along with the great debate regarding natural selection, and who came up with the theory first: Charles Darwin or Alfred Russel Wallace? Turns out, they both got there independently — although my hopes had been with Wallace, who spent far more time in the field.

I studied scientific classifications and became fascinated with odd hybrid combinations. For two animals to produce offspring, they must be genetically similar enough to belong to the same genus.

Ligers, Leopons and Tigards are the results of interbreeding between lions, leopards, and tigers. This can happen because all these cats belong to the genus *Panthera*. Similarly, horses, zebras and donkeys, who all belong to the genus *Equus*, can produce mules, zonkeys and zebroids.

Humans and chimpanzees belong to the same family, *Hominidae*, but different genus, so they could never interbreed. But humans could — and did — breed with at least two other early hominins, Neanderthals and Denisovans, who share the *Homo* genus with us.

By the time I was thirteen, I would often sneak onto our roof on hot summer nights and listen to the lions. In my daydreams, I followed the old Arab Slave Route into the heart of Africa with Richard Francis Burton and John Hanning Speke, as we tried to find the source of the Nile.

Or I pretended I was Henry Morton Stanley, braving the skull-shaped continent of Africa alone, in search of Doctor David Livingstone. Truth be told, I preferred to imagine myself as Dr. Livingstone, who got famously lost on purpose. He had vowed never to quit exploring, and even after being "found" by Stanley, did not return to England.

I thought I was getting scientifically modern when I began avidly watching *In Search Of;* and listened breathlessly as Leonard Nimoy put forward evidence for all sorts of unexplained phenomena. You can imagine, I was drawn particularly to episodes about the missing link, stories of yetis in Nepal, or bigfoots roaming the Pacific Northwest.

And when the first *Indiana Jones* movie came out, I was instantly hooked — even though he was an archaeologist, not a naturalist, and seemed to run from animals more than observe them.

Indy was hot on the trail of adventure, and I wanted to follow.

How I wish I'd asked Mr. Smith when and where he'd taken the photo. Did *he* even take it, or did someone give him the negative? Had he stood before that mighty gorilla like I yearned to?

I'd never met anyone who'd gone to Africa or seen any kind of ape in the wild, but I had a burning desire to do just that. One evening, while sitting on the roof listening to the lions, I vowed that one day I would go to the steamy jungle where the apes lived and see one for myself.

Lar Gibbon (*Hylobates lar*).
Habitat: Tropical broadleaf forest. Range: Southern Asia.

Chapter Three

Papillion
(1985)

*E*ight years later, I finally hit the road in search of adventure, and hopefully, an ape or two. I had a Canon AE-1 camera and plenty of slide film. Plus, a duffle bag crammed with clothes and a burning desire to see the world.

That first time away from home, I kept on the move. While gone, I crossed forty countries in a year and a half. My two biggest challenges were staying clothed and fed. Three months in, someone stole the duffle bag with all my clothes, and at about the same time, my money began to run out.

But I was infatuated with travel and new places and the odd characters I met on the road. In some ways, I was not just emotionally but physically unable to go home, as if my core itself would resist a return to domestic life. Not now, it whispered, you just got started! I just couldn't leave the open road.

You might say I developed ecophobia, the fear of home. But in my case, it was only not wanting to go home, not a fear of the actual place.

I felt connected to Dr. Livingstone and could hear him adamantly telling Stanley that he had no intention of giving up exploration and returning to civilization. "I will go anywhere provided it is forward!" he had said. This coming from a sixty-year-old man with almost no teeth.

So, I found work as I went, and I was willing to do almost anything: I swung a sledgehammer for ten dollars a day in Israel, washed mountains of dishes in London, and even rewired the electrical system in a brothel in Newcastle, Australia. I bartended, worked on construction sites, and taught English, too.

I also sent home ethnic jewelry to be sold at my hometown coffee shop, and I began submitting travel articles to several New Hampshire newspapers.

Anything that enabled me to remain abroad. Remain free.

Just like Elsa the lioness. Well, maybe not exactly like that, but you get my drift.

And I learned how to get by on very little. I scrounged and saved. I obtained secondhand clothes and washed and mended them myself. I hid the few dollars I had saved in a secret lining of my belt and only spent it in emergencies. I slept in shacks, on rooftops, and on beat-up couches. I used local transport, and whenever possible, I walked. I skipped meals and sometimes went a whole day without food.

Things slowed down dramatically once I reached Thailand — not that I had a say in it.

I had gotten in a motorcycle accident and was forced to recuperate in a hammock for six weeks while the road rash healed.

On the island of Koh Samui, in the Gulf of Thailand, I rented a palm-thatched bungalow for two dollars a day. It featured a simple bed made from bamboo and a thin mattress under a worn mosquito net. It had no electricity, but there was a small porch that looked out over the turquoise sea with two bamboo chairs and a rickety table.

The complex had a half-dozen huts and a small restaurant and was run by a nice couple with two young daughters of nine or ten. When I limped into their reception area, they were horrified by the bloody splotches on my Thai string pants. My left leg was one long scab from my ankle to my hip, and every time I bent it, which I could not entirely avoid, the scabs cracked and bled.

The father—a man named Bon— helped me to my bungalow with paternal care. He removed the table from the porch and set up a hammock for me.

He also brought me a collection of dilapidated novels left by other travelers. Half of them were in German or French, but I gladly pulled two English novels—*Papillon* and *Zen and the Art of Motorcycle Maintenance*—out of the mix.

The restaurant was just a stone's throw away, but too far for me to limp. Bon instructed his two daughters to watch over me. All I had to do was raise my fingers and make one of two signs, and within a few minutes, they'd bring me either a dish of pad Thai or a banana shake. It all went on a tab, but even after eating four or five meals daily—and drinking almost countless banana shakes—I found I still lived for under five dollars a day.

Despite my injuries, I was overjoyed with a sense of being free. With the sea breeze came an uplifting conviction that all things were possible, and the salty aroma of the sea mixed with odors that floated over from the kitchen intoxicated me.

The restaurant entrance was only thirty feet away, but during my first week, I never made it that far. From my hammock, I observed large breakers hurtling seaweed and driftwood onto the sand, but I never made it to the water either.

Instead, I read a lot while my body healed.

I watched monitor lizards lumber by.

I observed macaque monkeys raiding my neighboring bungalows for food.

The days blended into each other so smoothly that I hardly noticed their passing.

It would have been paradise except for the gibbon.

A troop of Lar gibbons (*Hylobates lar*) inhabited the coconut groves around our bungalow complex. They swooped through the trees in the cool mornings with their whooping calls echoing clearly through the crisp air.

These apes are the fastest and most agile of all tree-dwelling, non-flying mammals. Their feet and hands are elongated, and their wrists are designed with a ball and socket joint that allows them to use very little energy when swinging from limb to limb.

When I first arrived, I was enchanted by them, and as I gently swayed in my hammock, I listened to them communicate with one another. You can hear them from over a half-mile away, their voices clear and powerful.

The only apes in Thailand are gibbons. There used to be orangutans, but agriculture, logging and palm oil plantations destroyed much of their habitat. You'd have to go to Malaysia or Indonesia to find them now.

Gibbons are social animals who mate for life. Couples will vocalize together, singing duets that are occasionally joined by their young. Males boast ownership of their territories through song and sing solos in the hopes of attracting a mate. Each song is so unique that it can be used to identify the area from which the gibbon comes.

One morning, after I had been on the island for about a week, I realized that I hadn't heard the gibbons. I also didn't hear the waves, which meant the tide was out, and the silence that blanketed the beach seemed ominous.

While I listened intently, my eyes drifted to the restaurant. There, in the shade of a large banyan tree, I noticed a lone gibbon sitting on the ground.

I grabbed my camera on which I'd already affixed the zoom lens and focused on the small ape.

He had tan fur; the tips highlighted golden when he leaned forward into a shaft of morning light. His small ears just about disappeared into the furry head. His face was dark, with two large, black eyes. Of course, he was tailless—apes don't have tails—but other than that, he looked more like a monkey than an ape.

He reminded me of the gibbon I'd often visited at Capron Park when I was a kid living in Attleboro. The one named Vanilla.

I smiled, excited to see a gibbon only thirty feet away. But then I spied the rope tied to a collar around his neck.

Apparently, someone had captured him and left him there, probably as a lure for travelers passing by the complex.

I took my finger off the shutter-release button and lowered the camera. I felt sick to my stomach. My own freedom was my most valued possession. How could they keep such a beautiful animal captive?

I picked up my camera again and focused on the gibbon's face.

And what can I say I really saw there? In the past, we were told that we should not anthropomorphize animals, meaning we shouldn't attribute human behavior or emotions to their actions. But when I looked in that gibbon's eyes, I saw worry and sadness as clearly as if I was looking at someone I knew well.

If we don't anthropomorphize, we tend to shrug off the pain or discomfort an animal might feel. We might assign them an inferior mind. Much of this perspective stems from the writings of 17th-century philosopher René Descartes who declared that only humans are conscious and have a brain that lets them be self-aware. This became a chief justification for the disregard of animal well-being.

The philosophers of that era concluded that the nature of an animal's consciousness could never be truly known—for that matter, it can't even be proven to exist. Descartes thought of animals as "automata." But we know differently now. For over a hundred years, scientists have been studying animal consciousness, and many species exhibit emotion-like behavior and awareness in ways traditionally only ascribed to humans.

And why shouldn't animals be conscious and aware? Mammals and birds both possess the neurological framework needed to generate consciousness. In humans, that lead to sentience, subjectivity, and the power to distinguish the relationship between oneself and the environment.

Why not in animals? Or at least the apes who resemble us so much.

I was lost in thought about what was going through the captive gibbon´s mind when Franco showed up on my porch.

Franco was from Mexico. He was in his mid-thirties, with a full black beard lined with streaks of silver that matched his hair. He lived in the bungalow next door.

He looked at the gibbon. *"No es bueno,"* he said and shook his head.

Suddenly we heard another gibbon call out. There was a sadness to the call.

The captive gibbon looked in that direction anxiously. He tried to inhale a gulp of air and inflate his throat sac, but the collar impeded him. A desperate look of panic filled his eyes.

He exhaled, unable to reply to the call.

Franco stormed over to the restaurant. He gestured at one of the young girls and said, "Go get Bon. I need to talk to your papa."

Over the next few days, the ape was the focus of the conversation between my neighbors and the young girls who brought my banana shakes. The owner, Bon, considered the gibbon good luck. He said he would never hurt him, and someday he would most definitely set it free.

But not now.

We liked Bon. He was friendly and helpful. None of the travelers wanted to offend him, but we all agreed the ape must be set free.

I'd started reading *Papillion*, an autobiographical novel written by Henri Charrière about his time in a penal colony in French Guiana. Charrière spent most of his sentence in solitary confinement, planning his escapes. He was eventually sent to secluded Devil's Island, which was considered inescapable.

As I read, I felt the gibbon's eyes on me, watching curiously from the shadows. He reminded me of how the prisoners in *Papillion* watched the guards, and I eventually began to call the ape Papillion.

Sometimes he walked around bipedally like a human, with his arms raised over his head, but mostly he sat in the tree and stared off into nowhere.

I felt that my injuries and lack of mobility, and the rope and collar tied to his neck, united us.

We were doing time together.

From my hammock I glared at the rope that ran from Papillion's collar to the tree. The banyan was huge — about ten feet wide with roots sprawling everywhere — and the rope was tied off to a lower root.

I decided that as soon as I was able to limp to the tree, I'd either untie the rope, or cut it, and set Papillion free. That thought got me through the next few days.

But Bon must have anticipated someone doing exactly that because I woke one morning to see that the far end of the rope had been retied high up in the tree.

Daily, Franco confronted Bon, and every day he was given excuses.

"I need this gibbon here to scare the snakes away," Bon said. The restaurant had a trash pile behind it, and that attracted rats, and they, in turn, attracted the snakes.

Over the coming days I did hear Papillion shriek when he saw a snake, but he only scampered up the tree — he had no intention of going near the serpent.

Franco noticed this also and determinedly argued that point.

After a week, I began wading into the water for a half-hour each day to let the salt heal my wounds. I just stood there and let the saltwater swirl around me while I stared inland, careful not to disturb my scabs with big movements.

At first it hurt like hell, but after a few days, I noticed a change. I was healing.

Despite the pain, my heart surged with the wind and the sea breeze, and I felt the magic of the place. I was in paradise.

Until my eyes strayed to Papillion sitting there placidly.

One day, as I stood waist-deep in the water, Franco waded out to join me looking out to sea. He told me about his discussion with Bon.

We turned and faced the palm-lined beach, coconut groves extending inland, and the slender trees danced with the breeze. Franco said, "Bon claims the gibbon is a magical creature. The Taoists apparently believe that gibbons live hundreds of years. He actually said to me, 'What matter is a few days on a rope to a creature that lives that long — especially if it helps me bring in more tourists?'"

Franco furrowed his heavy brows and said, "I told him this would only make people not want to stay here."

I thought he was right. Over the next few days, more and more travelers took notice, and a few complained.

In the mornings, I swayed in my hammock and stared at Papillon. I thought of my own freedom and wondered how I would deal with captivity. I was restless because of my injury, yet I was free to go. But I missed my family terribly, and I wondered whether the gibbon missed his family as well – they seemed to hover around us, calling out but never venturing within sight.

I knew gibbons formed long-term bonds, and I pondered what he yearned for more, his freedom or his mate. The more I thought about it, the more I decided that both were intertwined.

Finally, I was mended enough to take meals in the restaurant.

I joined Franco at a table, and before long, Bon approached me with a wide smile. "You are getting better," he said.

I smiled. "I am."

"Is there anything you need?" asked Bon.

I gave Franco a grin, nodded at the gibbon, and said, "Let the ape go."

Bon sighed. "You too?" he asked.

And after I nodded again, he said, "When the gibbons are around, they keep the macaques away — they are dirty animals that steal food from the tables."

Franco nodded, "Then feed him a few bananas when he comes around. If he likes you, he will stay. And then he can help chase away the monkeys without being a prisoner."

Bon stared at us for a long moment, then sighed and nodded his head.

He stepped into the kitchen and grabbed a banana, then stood by the base of the tree.

He whistled, and Papillon timidly dropped to the ground, one arm extended toward the fruit. As the gibbon hesitantly leaned toward the banana, Bon quickly reached forward and flipped open a small metal clasp on the collar. The collar dropped to the ground with a clink.

Papillion stepped back, the banana forgotten, and in a flash, he was up the tree. A second later he was gone, swinging silently through the canopy.

The next day's sunrise found me sitting in a chair on my porch. I was leaning back with my feet up on the railing and stared at the horizon.

My morning had been saddened by an article in the *Bangkok Post* about the death of Dian Fossey, who had been murdered a few months before in the Virunga volcanoes region of Zaire. The article had new details on her murderers, although everyone already knew who had done it—poachers.

For an hour I watched a tiny green lizard eat mosquito after mosquito while I thought of the woman who'd spent so much of her life trying to protect the mountain gorillas—only to die at the hands of poachers.

Suddenly the cool dawn silence was broken by a gibbon's call, and soon that was answered by another. Other members of the family joined in, and before long, I heard a jumble of different voices.

One of those voices I hadn't heard in a while. I smiled as I realized it was Papillion's.

Papillion was free at last. Just like in the novel, I thought.

I watched the treetops until I spotted Papillion perched in the upper branches of a coconut tree. I suddenly realized that in all the time I'd been watching him, I'd never taken his photo.

I zoomed in with my camera, but even with the zoom, the gibbon only showed up as a small dot.

I took the photo anyway, my first one of an ape.

"Go live it up," I said with a smile as he swooped away.

A few weeks later, I was finally well enough to leave. I said goodbye to Franco and Bon and my other bungalow neighbors, shouldered my backpack, and went to the restaurant for a final meal.

While I enjoyed a bowl of pad Thai, I noticed some movement by the trash pile out behind the restaurant. Peering into the shadows, I made out a raptor of some kind perched on top of a pole that had been driven down into the trash pile.

A cable was attached from the bird's leg to the pole.

I stepped closer and saw it was a fish eagle with a white belly.

He was eyeing a snake slithering by beneath him, and, with a screech, dropped on it.

Bon appeared next to me with a broad grin.

"See," he said, "soon, no more snake problem."

I was about to say something when Franco appeared by my side.

He glanced at the eagle as it gulped down the snake, and then at Bon, and said, "We need to talk again."

Koh Samui, Thailand. 1985.

Common Chimpanzee (*Pan troglodytes*).
Habitat: Tropical forest and savannas. Range: Equatorial Africa.

Chapter Four

Gorilas en la Niebla
(1988)

A defiant roar shook me. I cringed in the darkness. It was a mountain gorilla's cry; even having never encountered one, I recognized it from documentaries I'd seen. It boomed in my head. I tried to look up at it, but my eyes were painfully sensitive to the impossibly bright light coming from that direction.

I clamped them shut. I passed out.

I woke later, and in a dimmer light, realized I was in a movie theater. My mind slowly churned until it finally focused.

I was in Panama — Panama City.

The movie's credits were running on the screen, but the theatre was empty, and the air conditioning had been shut off.

The heat was sweltering.

My shirt was soaked with sweat. I felt certain that a sickness had taken hold of me. A repulsive stench alerted me to the fact that I had thrown up on my chest while I was unconscious.

It was all too much. I closed my eyes again and let my mind drift away, anywhere but here.

I remembered crossing the Brownsville border into Mexico.

A barrage of images from the following six months flashed before my inner eye.

Pithecophilia

There are no apes in Central America. No gorillas, only *guerillas* - freedom fighters or insurgents, depending on your stance. In Guatemala, I met some cheerful retired rebels who bought me round after round of beer. It was a different story in Honduras. The Contras—who had temporarily fled Nicaragua—shot at me as I sped by in my truck, blowing out a back window.

But overall, I enjoyed the mellow pace of the Latin lands. Having my own vehicle made me independent, and that was priceless.

My Nissan pickup had a king cab and camper shell, a tape deck that worked, and lots of Jimmy Buffet cassettes. I traveled with a few crates of supplies and a stove to cook meals, and I slept in the back of the truck whenever possible.

I was also earning travel money now by writing about my journeys for several New Hampshire newspapers, and had gotten Olympus and Eastern Mountain Sports to sponsor me with cameras and gear.

From Brownsville, I went south to Veracruz, then hugged the coast up and around the Yucatan before entering Belize and northern Guatemala.

At the Tikal ruins, I camped by one of the jungle-covered towers and woke to the deep bark of a black howler monkey (*Alouatta pigra*).

Howlers are one of the loudest terrestrial animals in the world. They can grow to three feet, but to hear that powerful, creaking howl descend from the canopy, you'd think they were eight feet tall and full of muscle.

Several of them eventually skirted through the trees above me, staying within sight while I watched from my tailgate and enjoyed my morning coffee. They move quadrupedally, always grasping with at least two limbs. Their prehensile tails are long and powerful. They can actually grab fruit with them while they are on the go.

When they moved on, I tried to shadow them, hoping to catch a better glimpse, but they appeared aware of my efforts and simply disappeared into the deep canopy when I got close.

Eventually, I found myself in Nicaragua, and when I passed through Managua, it became impossible to ignore the violence. On the side of the road, a burnt-out husk of a school bus glared at me. In the back window, a yellow dress fluttered on broken glass.

I was traveling with a Swiss painter called Vendu. He spoke a little English, but our conversations were still fairly basic.

"These people are chimps," he said.

I realized he was comparing chimpanzees with the bombers of the school bus — in this case, the Contras — but in my eyes, it was an unfair comparison.

Chimpanzees have a terrible reputation because of attacks on humans, but these acts are usually committed by captive apes or ones raised as pets. In the wild, they rarely attack people. They are afraid of us.

Aggression is indeed a common part of chimpanzee behavior. Males will kill other males when they are warring with other groups. They sometimes kill their young, too, if they feel it is not their offspring, but they are not deranged killers.

Chimps that are held in cages can become quite vicious, and there are more than a few chimpanzee researchers who are missing parts of their fingers. Good for the chimps, I say; we shouldn't keep any ape in a cage.

But the worst cases of attacks on humans by chimpanzees are committed by what are called free-ranging chimps.

These are chimpanzee pets that live alongside humans, and often the apes have health issues. In one horrible case that I read, the ape that attacked its owner was later found to have Lyme's disease and that its owner had been feeding it Xanax.

In humans, the overuse of Xanax can cause mood swings and lead to violent or aggressive behavior. And who knows the pain the chimp experienced by having untreated Lyme's disease.

Rather than tell Vendu all this, I pretended he was comparing the work of the rebels to a demented pet chimp, and that might not have been far off.

We continued south through Costa Rica, where we camped along the Nicoya Peninsula. There were no rebels there, and we truly relaxed. But for the rest of my time in Central America, I continuously pondered chimpanzees, their nature, and how dangerous they might be.

Much of the research done by Jane Goodall shows that chimpanzees can be downright Machiavellian, plotting and scheming against each other.

And a quote by Goodall that challenged my stance on how harmless chimps were kept returning to me. Witnessing the total annihilation of one group of chimpanzees by another, she wrote, "If they had firearms and had been taught to use them, I suspect that they would have used them to kill."

Thoughts of Vendu brought me back to the movie theater in Panama City, where I was delirious and sick. It seemed I had been there for a long time, and it was only near the end of that afternoon that I regained enough of my senses to realize the film had played through at least twice.

I focused on the movie, and for the first time, I realized the actors were speaking in Spanish. I smiled through cracked lips at the irony when I realized what was playing. *Gorilas en la Niebla*, or Gorillas in the Mist, is the story of Dian Fossey's time with the mountain gorillas of the Virunga volcanic chain of eastern Africa.

And for one graceful moment, I forgot my state and watched Fossey — played by Sigourney Weaver — in one of her first encounters with gorillas. It seemed so wonderful that I tried to imagine myself there, in her place, feeling the rain falling on me, smelling the moist earth and the dripping green vegetation, and communing with the gorillas.

I wanted so desperately to be anywhere but in that theater.

I remembered my old photo of the mountain gorilla and tried to lose myself in it.

But my condition refused to let me be, and after several hours of convalescing in the theater, I knew I had to leave.

My stomach churned.

I heard a noise in the hallway and slunk lower in my seat.

I had only a vague recollection of the last few days: Panama in turmoil, sweltering under a heatwave while a hepatitis epidemic swept through the city. There were riots. Angry mobs were torching vehicles and smashing storefront windows.

What were they rioting over? Something about the U.S. returning the canal. I wasn't sure, and I didn't care. I just wanted to get out of the country, and for a week, Vendu and I tried to get on a plane or boat to South America.

We had no luck. And during the next few days, the safest part of the city had been reduced to two city blocks, which were surrounded by guards and barricades.

Angry protestors threw rocks from the other side of the dividers, and we steered clear of them, not wanting to get hit.

I remember waking that morning, weak with a dry mouth. Vendu's backpack leaned against the wall, but he wasn't around. I staggered into the hotel lobby to find the place deserted.

As in a dream, I walked out into the street, squinting and barely able to see in what seemed an unbearably bright light. I stumbled down the road over broken glass and debris. I felt like I was in a post-apocalyptic world.

That's when I heard the roar. I squinted and slowly registered that a livid mob was heading in my direction.

I turned to run and almost immediately collided with a signpost. I fell, gripping my forehead, but fear pushed me back to my feet.

I fled, almost blindly, just trying to get away, until I came upon the movie theater. The lobby was empty, and I glanced around in panic. I heard glass breaking and ducked into one of the theaters where a movie was playing to an empty room.

I crouched down low in a seat, trying to look invisible, and passed out.

Images of butchered gorillas finally drove me out of the theater. My fevered body ached. In the back of my mind, I thought I heard a fire alarm blaring for the last hour, but when I left the theater, the lobby was silent.

On the street, windows had been smashed, and several cars were on fire. I watched two looters pry back the protective grid on a shop front and crawl in.

My eyes were extremely sensitive to light. To open them, even a crack, was to expose myself to a blinding glitter.

I stood there for I don't know how long. Numb.

I began to stumble in the direction of my hotel when I heard a great shout from a block away. I was feverish and barely present. My first thought was it sounded like the roar of a howler monkey.

I continued, holding my arms in front of me. I could barely see where I was going.

And then, from about a block away, I heard shouts.

If I were a gazelle, or some type of antelope, I'd have gotten away clear and free right then. Most ungulates are ruled by instinct and don't appear to debate whether they should run or not. Time is precious when you are prey, and the antelope that pauses to ponder its situation is the one most likely to be eaten.

If I had been a swift-hooved animal, I wouldn't have thought about the mob until about five big leaps after I was first spooked, and with that head start, I would have lost them.

But unfortunately, I am a human (*Homo sapiens*), descended from a common ancestor of the chimpanzee, and we don't just run off like the whimsical antelope. We watch and observe. We gather information using our unique cognitive abilities so we can make informed decisions.

We weigh costs and benefits.

We decide whether it's going to be Fight or Flight.

So, when the mob spotted me slowly ambling away, I didn't run.

I gawked at it, feebly trying to think my way through the situation.

The dense group of people drew closer, and I could see some were armed with sticks.

I ducked into an alley, but it was too late.

I wish I could tell you it all ended well, but I can't.

Thankfully, I have only a few memories of the next two weeks.

The mob closing in... later, stumbling lost in the city... then waking in a hotel room covered in my own fluids.

Eventually, I somehow got on a flight out of the country and stumbled into a hospital in Quito, Ecuador.

When I regained my faculties, I remember watching, yellow-eyed, from my hospital bed, as Noriega shook a sword at the cameras while angry spectators cheered him on. I was glued to the screen, hoping to catch a glance of Vendu. To this day, I don't know what happened to him.

And I wondered who was acting like an animal here. Can we chase each other in mobs, beat and kill each other, and still call ourselves civilized? Do we, as a species, make good, conscious decisions?

After millennia of forks on the great branching tree of life, did we come all this way just to make war the inevitable product of our human uniqueness?

It appeared to me that using our consciousness to constantly think only about ourselves, and what benefits us, is not a very noble use of it at all.

It would be a while before I craved the companionship of my fellow man.

The next time I hit the road, I decided to steer clear of interactions with people and instead seek out an ape encounter. I would get as deep into the wild as I could, and maybe there I would have the experience I have yearned for all these years.

I closed my eyes and pretended I was a gazelle.

Sumatran Orangutan (*Pongo abelii*).
Habitat: Tropical forest and jungle. Range: Northern Sumatra, Indonesia.

Chapter Five

Men of the Forest
(1991)

*T*he trail skirted a roaring river, and on the other side, monkeys were howling in the trees. I listened intently, but their call wasn't a distinctive one I knew—like a gibbon's—and I couldn't identify them.

For nearly a week I had been following a path that ran parallel to Sumatra's Gunung Leuser National Park. At night I stayed in modest villages with minimal accommodations, glad for shelter from the rain that rarely let up—and then in the morning, I was back on the muddy trail.

It wasn't always clear that I was on a footpath connecting the villages on the outskirts of a park that encompassed more than three thousand square miles. Sometimes the track forked, and it often veered into the dense tropical rainforest where the jungle closed around me.

I always let out a great sigh of relief when I stumbled into a village at the end of the day.

But now, the muddy path was looking more like a game trail, and I seriously questioned whether I should keep going. Dense clouds loomed over the tops of the hills, which I passed, so I couldn't steer by the sun. I hadn't seen a sign or another human for almost four hours. It was off-season, and because of the rains I saw virtually no other travelers, not even Indonesian visitors.

The river had mellowed a bit here, and by a quiet pool I stopped to get a drink.

As I bent over the water, cupping my hands, I caught my haggard reflection. I was shocked by the wild look in my eyes, and — as so often — my thoughts drifted to apes. Over the last few years, I have realized that I suffer from pithecophilia, a "love of apes and monkeys," and they're never far from my mind.

I stared at my reflection and pondered it. One quality that many people mistakenly take as strictly human is our ability to recognize ourselves in a mirror. Cats don't seem to know themselves when they look into a mirror, and they couldn't be bothered to investigate it any further. A dog will interact with its reflection as if it is another dog, trying to scare off their mirror image as if it were an intruder, or play with it, depending on their nature.

These social responses are easy to understand because, at first glance, it is what appears to be. The primary concern for most animals is to discern whether they are in danger, so there is an urgency to figure that out fast.

Apes are different. Greater apes like chimpanzees, gorillas and orangutans initially act like they are confronting another ape, but soon they realize they are controlling the image. This leads to a behavior where they figure out this is not another ape by making movements in front of the mirror while watching themselves.

What do they do next? Just what a human would do. They carefully clean their teeth and eyes, and then examine parts of their bodies that they normally can't see — like their butts.

I stared at my reflection for a moment longer, and then smiled and moved my head, just to be certain it was me.

And then it began to rain again, just a light sprinkle at first, but it was building. The humidity clung to me like a desperate creature.

When I left the water's edge, the trail disappeared into the densest wall of vegetation I'd ever seen. The trees around me were giants, with buttressed roots, that soared upward, transforming into massive trunks that split into thick, moss-covered branches.

An ancient vine, its base nearly three feet thick, had a stranglehold on one of them.

Out of sight in the canopy, birds sang loudly, but then a thunderclap cast them in silence.

I listened to the thunder rumble over the jungle-clad hills. It sounded like a tiger's low growl. The vibrations seemed to shake the water from the trees.

I felt a surge of panic sweep over me, but kept my head down, following what was left of the trail. I thought of apes again to divert myself from my rising fear.

The fact that apes can recognize their own reflection suggests that they possess a concept of *self*. And knowing your self is a prerequisite to understanding the minds of others.

But they haven't seemed to evolve beyond this point, at least as far as mirrors are concerned. They use the mirror for basic functions only. Apes have never been observed communicating or signaling with a mirror, or changing their appearance. For a bit, I wondered how similar an ape's mind might be to my own, but deep down, I knew I was trying not to admit that I might have taken a wrong turn.

I stopped and looked around.

Initially, I had been relieved when the trail took me under the canopy, and I thought I would escape the rain with a roof of thick green obscuring the sky.

But the track I'd been following kept diminishing.

Now it did look like game trail—and a seldom-used one at that.

At this point, I began to doubt that the path I was on would lead to the next village. But there wasn't enough daylight left to backtrack, so I decided to push on for another hour, in the hope of finding a semblance of civilization after all.

You may think my aimless plodding to be reckless, and I suppose you're right. But on this trip, I'd already been traveling for over a year, and my general confidence in my ability to find my way—and survive somehow if I didn't—knew few limits.

Pithecophilia

For six months, I had explored northern India, Nepal and Thailand, and then spent another six months in Australia, hitch-hiking from Darwin down to Sydney, where I worked for a while trying to replenish my funds.

Now I was back on the road!

I was still writing travel articles for the New Hampshire newspapers: *The Telegraph* out of Nashua, and *The Hollis Times*. *The Hollis Times* was my hometown paper, and they only paid twenty-five dollars an article, but I received about five hundred dollars per feature from *The Telegraph*. They'd bought six features from my last trip to Central America and had committed to another six features from Asia.

Not a bad gig, I thought. I traveled on a budget of four to five hundred dollars per month, and one feature would cover that. But I also had to pay for flights, so I picked up odd jobs whenever and wherever I could.

After working in a bar in Sydney for a stint, I was financially recharged and ready to spend the next six months exploring Asia. I wanted to get as deep into the jungle as I could. I had an unquenchable desire to immerse myself in it.

So far, in Sumatra, I was getting by with a few phrases of the local dialect and a fundamental understanding of chess. I chatted with the locals I encountered on the trails, and I knew how to negotiate a price for a hut or a bed if one was available.

Each night, just after the sky darkened, I would be summoned by the village chief to play a game of chess while the villagers looked on. I thought I was a reasonably good player, but these quiet, old, bare-chested men in Sumatra quickly dispatched me.

It was always done politely, and the next day when I hit the trail again, I was often fondly waving goodbye to the friendly people that I knew for just one night.

I stopped, crouched on the trail, and ate a banana. I knew I was in a tight spot as the afternoon sun was waning. The treetops stretched a hundred feet above me, and the last rays of the sun were still lighting the uppermost branches, but I was cast in gloom.

The trail, if you could call it that anymore, was so muddy now that at times I sank six inches into the muck. The only consolation was that I could probably follow my tracks back if I had to under better lighting in the morning.

As long as it didn't rain harder and wash them away. I stared at my boot prints and noticed a leech, slowly inching my way.

I had hoped to avoid the rain when I moved underneath the trees but now saw that the water ran right off the canopy, occasionally striking me in fat, heavy drops. The massive trunks rippled with streams of water flowing down the thick, sprawling roots. When I looked closer at one trunk, a foot-long centipede scurried past.

Bamboo and thick shrubs obscured my line of sight at ground level. Vines as thick as my legs were dangling from the heavens. Wet plants steamed from the heat, and I was dripping with sweat and rainwater.

I carried little in my pack, but it was drenched and weighed on my shoulders. I set it by my side to assess my options again. It was pointless to go on; I would only end up getting myself even more lost in the coming night.

I needed to find a place where I could spend the night. I scanned around for a tree to climb, but there were either towering giants with no lower limbs or stunted, secondary growth trees, starved of sunlight, rotting and ready to collapse.

I dug through my pack and took stock: one pair of jeans, a sarong and change of underwear, another t-shirt, one candy bar and an orange, a candle and some damp matches, and a novel, *The Power of Myth* by Joseph Campbell.

I'm going to be hungry by tomorrow, I thought.

I did have a small flashlight with me, but I had used up the batteries a few nights before while reading in bed.

I hadn't seen any trees with fruit and didn't know if I should dare to forage until I was desperate. An orangutan would, I thought. They will eat just about any kind of fruit, but their diet also consists of bird eggs, insects, honey and certain types of tree bark.

Nightfall slowly descended on the jungle; shadows were thickening. My mind raced with ape trivia, which usually calmed me.

I remembered that Tarzan made it to Sumatra in book #22 of the Edgar Rice Burroughs series, *Tarzan and the Foreign Legion*. The storyline was okay, but I didn't like how Burroughs depicted the Japanese soldiers; he published it the year World War II ended.

Of course, Tarzan held his own against Asia's wild animals, just as he did in Africa.

As a boy I'd been surprised to learn that Sumatra had many of the same wild animals found in Africa: elephants, rhinos, leopards and big snakes. The only difference seemed to be that they had tigers instead of lions in Sumatra.

But I recalled nothing from the novel that might offer a clue to surviving. In the story, Tarzan seemed to baffle a Royal Air Force colonel as well when he "stripped to a loincloth and threw away his weapons."

But Burrough's depiction of the primal, primitive forest was apt.

It seemed like at any moment, a *Gigantopithecus* might step out of the shadows. That great ape—now extinct—was related to the orangutan and shared the subfamily *Ponginae.* As I stared into the gloom, I felt if there was ever a place where a last *Gigantopithecus* might still be lingering, this was it.

I wondered how I would react to a thirteen-hundred-pound primate, standing nearly ten feet tall, stepping out of the thicket.

I struggled to think of something else. I was scared enough already.

In the seventeenth and eighteenth centuries, Europeans became acquainted with chimpanzees, gorillas and orangutans during colonial expansion and the opening of trade routes through Africa and Southeast Asia.

The Dutch physician Jacobus Bonitius (1592-1631) described one female orangutan as large-breasted and furry, with a mane like a lion. Bonitius said the local name for the creature was *Ourang Outang* or "man of the forest," and that they could talk but refused for fear that they might be put to work.

Bonitius also suggested that orangutans lived in shelters and buried their dead, which I'm sure confused the experts of the day.

Modern scientists have discovered evidence of an early hominin species—*Homo naledi* (335,000-236,000 BP)—caring for their dead in South Africa. This is considered possible evidence of early religious experiences.

If orangutans acted upon a knowledge of death and its inevitability, that would put them in an entirely different class of being. However, no ape burial sites were ever discovered.

In 1809 the French naturalist Jean-Baptiste Lamarck (1744-1829) suggested man was descended directly from orangutans through transmutation—an idea that was quite scandalous at the time.

Then in 1855, Alfred Russel Wallace—one of my heroes—theorized that humans and orangutans were descended from a common ancestor, not that we were derived from orangutans.

We know now that humans and chimpanzees branched off from a common ancestor six million years ago, and that orangutans broke away eight million years before that. They are our far distant cousins.

All my life, I had yearned to encounter an orangutan, but with nightfall approaching, the thought seemed too scary. Sumatrans have taboos about hunting them or looking into their faces directly. And there are macabre folk tales that involve humans kidnapped by orangutans, and female orangutans seducing lost hunters.

I felt a shudder pass through me as I wondered what might have inspired those legends. Campbell's *Power of Myth* had my head spinning with stories of bizarre sacrifices and other extreme rituals.

I shook myself and glanced around.

And then my fear settled into a deeper level. Superstitions can surely make you edgy, but there were real threats that walked this jungle. I feared being trampled by an elephant or rhinoceros, but what filled me with absolute dread was the thought of encountering a tiger.

And yes, I do realize Tarzan fought off all those dangers in Sumatra, but that still didn't translate to anything helpful in my current situation.

An eerie glow settled over the jungle, and I knew soon I'd be left in the dark. Dense vegetation, a few feet taller than I, covered the ground. I listened to fat drops of rain hitting the broad leaves suspended above and around me.

I walked a dozen paces from the trail, searching for a tree I might climb. A voice in my head screamed not to leave the diminishing lifeline back to civilization.

Those few steps were enough to make me lose my nerve.

I stopped and fearfully glanced around.

I crouched there, catching my breath, when suddenly I realized the jungle had gone silent. Even the chatter of insects had stopped.

I held my breath.

I opened my ears and listened as hard as I could.

Even though I couldn't discern any movement or animal sounds, I *felt* the presence of something. My brain squeezed out one word—Tiger! My heart fluttered like a caged bird desperate to escape. The metallic taste of panic filled my mouth.

Silently, I reached forward and grabbed for a stick. My hands found one that was three feet long and about three inches thick but half-rotted.

I raised it to defend myself, but the jungle sounds slowly returned in the long moment that followed.

Crickets chirped... a fly buzzed past... I exhaled.

Then a twig snapped loudly. Several birds fluttered up to escape.

A bush shook violently twenty feet away—something large was coming my way, but I still couldn't see it.

When it was ten feet distance, I raised the stick, at first holding it pointed forward like a spear, but then I raised it over my head like a club.

I was determined not to go down without a fight.

And then, right in front of me, the bushes parted, and I was face to face with an orangutan.

The ape, an older female, had a large head with a prominent mouth.

She stared straight into my eyes, and I sensed that she was determining whether I was a threat or not.

Relief flooded my body like a deluge, and I collapsed to the ground. I lay in a heap, my arms shaking from adrenaline, while she observed me with a penetrating stare.

In the slow, timeless moment that followed, I watched the ape move to my side, nimbly bringing her bulky body closer until she stood next to me on bowed legs. She was covered with sparse, long, light reddish-brown hair over grey-black skin.

She nudged me with one long, curved finger, and then walked in a circle around me. I was still lying on the ground but managed to raise my head slightly and look at her.

I detected both a seasoned caution and a gentle inquisitiveness as she observed me, but nothing menacing. I was slowly coming around, my limbs again responding, and I raised myself to my elbows.

She paused for a moment and watched me, then continued slowly moving around me.

My first observation was that she was a fist-walker, not a knuckle-walker like a gorilla or a chimpanzee. I remembered that *Orang utan* meant "man of the forest" and as I watched what I thought was curiosity and concern in her eyes, I thought it a good name.

Was I anthropomorphizing again? Applying a human trait to an animal? I wasn't sure, but it seemed she smiled at me through her eyes.

She then made a cooing noise over her shoulder, and I heard more movement in the bushes. For the most part, apes in the wild converse vocally but non-verbally. They don't have words, but they can convey their general mood through sounds — even if they're not exactly spelling out how they feel. But words are unnecessary here. By combining facial expressions and gestures with sounds, they easily express intentions, warnings and desires.

More of them were approaching; I thought I detected excitement in their soft hooting calls. As I listened to the group converse, I imagined this probably wasn't too different from how our ancestors communicated in the far, dim past.

I wondered how life would be if I were limited to communicating only through guttural sounds, gestures and facial expressions.

The ruckus around me grew, and occasionally I'd get glimpses of them through the foliage. A group of orangutans is known as a congress, and over the next few minutes, I realized this congress was made up of about a dozen individuals.

At first only the mothers eyed me through the leaves. I could see three of them, and two had young clinging to them. For their first two years of life, infants have constant contact with their mothers, being carried, fed, and bedded by them.

Next, some of the juveniles ventured nearer. I guessed they were two or three years old. They didn't get closer than four feet but watched me openly.

When one of them moved even closer, the mothers began making sounds that told me they were nervous. That first female still stood by my side, and suddenly she sucked in air through pursed lips. I felt a rush of excitement as I recognized a "kiss squeak," which I had read about.

Quickly, the little ones faded into the brush, making soft hooting sounds as they retreated, and one of them blew a raspberry at me.

Within a minute, I was left alone in the once again silent jungle.

I stumbled back to my rapidly disappearing trail—my lifeline—and realized I only had a few minutes of light left to find a place for the night. With the orangutans gone, I suddenly felt incredibly lonely.

I was scared again.

But then I spotted a tree with a fat vine ascending from its base past a large, wide branch about fifteen feet above the ground. I scampered up and straddled the branch, trying to wedge myself against the trunk. I won't say I felt safe, but maybe a bit less vulnerable.

Peering through the trees, I detected a faint glow on the horizon. West, I thought. But at this point, knowing the direction was of little consequence. My best prospect seemed to try to backtrack in the morning. Assuming the rain didn't wash away my tracks.

The heat began to fade, and the buzzing of insects was drowning out all other sounds. It was deafening.

I once again imagined the wild animals that roamed this jungle, and once again, dread rose in my gut. The trees seemed just as overrun with life as the ground. It would only be a matter of time before a snake slithered past me.

A leech crawled onto my leg and I flicked it away.

I was terrified of falling out of the tree if I drifted off. I doubted I would sleep. I tried in vain to light my candle with my damp matches. If only I'd conserved the batteries in my flashlight.

I ate my last candy bar and leaned back the best I could, gripping the tree with my thighs and trying not to think about the long night ahead.

I had just reached the point where I couldn't see my hand in front of my face when I heard branches breaking. I nervously squinted and peered into the emptiness. Maybe it was just the orangutans returning, I told myself.

The thought that the orangutans were out there, somewhere, was the only thread of hope I held on to. I focused on it, trying to let the seconds pass, as I imagined them watching over me.

The noise continued to get closer and louder, and I wondered if this might be an elephant. Could it reach me?

And then I caught a flicker of light — the beam of a flashlight — and my heart started beating wildly. Humans! I thought excitedly.

Someone was walking down the path towards me. I could see several beams unsteadily sweeping the ground, getting closer.

Soon, five people dimly came into view in the shadows behind the lights. They walked slowly, their flashlights illuminating the trail just ahead of them.

"Excuse me," I said when the first one passed under my tree.

He jumped and pointed his flashlight up.

He smiled at me, but even with the bright beam of the light partially blinding me, I could see I had scared him.

"I thought you were a leopard," he said breathlessly.

"Nope, just an American," I said as I half-climbed, half-fell, out of the tree.

It turned out he was a guide. His name was Ian, and he was leading four Europeans on an adventure tour through the park. As luck would have it, they were camping a short distance away.

Ten minutes later, we entered a clearing where three tents had been erected with a rain trench around them. He checked the tents for snakes and assigned his clients two to a shelter — the third tent he would share with me. Ian said I could also share their meals tonight and tomorrow if I kicked in some money.

I had never been so happy to pay what amounted to about ten dollars for warm food. The cooked rice with carrots he prepared for us that night was one of the best meals I ever had.

He laughed when I told him of my village trek and informed me that I had taken a wrong turn a long way back. I was now in the heart of the national park, and the trail I'd lost was at least five hours away.

It had been a stressful day, and I was so relieved to have shelter. I slept like a log that night, not budging until Ian shook me awake the next morning.

We walked for nine hours that day. His clients were adrenaline junkies and welcomed any challenge before them. We followed a compass bearing for most of the day, climbing up jungle-clad ridges, grasping vines and exposed roots. I think even Tarzan would have been impressed.

I was dead-tired but didn't dare ask Ian to slow down. After all, he was leading me out of the jungle.

We stopped by a clear stream for a late lunch, and soon after that, we emerged from under the canopy. Finally, we crossed a suspension bridge that led into a small village on the other side.

I stopped on the bridge and looked back towards the jungle-covered mountains. Suddenly, thousands of bats poured out of the hills and into the gathering night.

The sight gave me the chills. But then I remembered the orangutans, and how they had inspected me and watched over me as I lay on the jungle floor.

I thought of the matriarch—the one who inquisitively circled me. I wished I could see her again. To be around her presence. When I'd been lost and clinging to the tree, the thought of her had comforted me.

And even now, for some strange reason, I felt she was still with me. I knew I would never forget her.

Mount Sibayak, Sumatra,
right before I got lost. 1991.

Mountain Gorilla (*Gorilla beringei beringei*).
Habitat: Montane cloud forest. Range: Central Africa.

Chapter Six

Oscar
(1993)

I was back in the jungle again, this time on the forested slopes of Mount Sabyinyo, a dormant volcano in Zaire's Virunga range. The range is comprised of eight major volcanoes and marks the border between Rwanda, Uganda and Zaire, which is now the Democratic Republic of the Congo.

Ancient hagenia trees crouched in the thick mist, their limbs draped with bearded lichens, and I crouched below them, waiting for my guide to return. The constant drizzle was a reminder that this place received seventy-two inches of rain a year.

I shivered in my wet clothing. Yesterday´s six-mile hike into the mountains, to base camp, had left my jeans and boots covered with mud. And this morning we'd hiked hard for an hour to get to this elevation — around nine thousand feet.

I was flush with sweat when we stopped.

Around me, a myriad of tiny orchids soaked in the moisture and the feeble sunlight that diffused through the jungle canopy down to the mossy jungle floor.

Visibility was limited to about thirty feet and dropped to just a few feet when the clouds blew in. But when it's clear, the view was magnificent. Or at least, so I'd been told; I hadn't seen the sun in ten days.

My guide claimed that on a clear day, you could see the smoking cones of Mount Nyiragongo and Mount Nyamu-ragira, twenty-five miles to the southwest. I had no interest in going there; of the eight volcanoes in the range, those are the only two that have no apes.

Just south of us, only fourteen miles away, stood Mount Bisoke, with mighty Karisimbi behind it, the highest of this range at 14,787 feet. I desperately wanted to see Bisoke. On the slopes of that mountain lay an alpine meadow called Kabara that was rich in history.

Three people whom I had read about for years had all crossed paths in that quiet meadow, although they were never there at the same time. Carl Akeley was there in 1921, George Schaller in 1959, and Dian Fossey in 1967.

Akeley was a naturalist collecting specimens for the American Museum of Natural History. Schaller was a zoologist and the first to study the apes that live there. Fossey was also a zoologist who conducted the first long-term study.

Sabyinyo, the mountain I was currently on, is the oldest in the volcanic range and rises 11,923 feet above sea level. I never thought I'd be this high, or this cold, in Africa.

It's no wonder these mountains have been shrouded in mystery for so long. They are a world unto themselves. Akeley described the Virungas as a place "... so fantastic and strange that you would not be surprised if you saw gnomes and fairies among the trees."

The Carthaginian explorer Hanno the Navigator reportedly found strange creatures in West Africa in the sixth or fifth century BC. He brought a few of them back and had their skins nailed to the walls of the Temple of Baal. And on several occasions the poor animals were slaughtered in the Roman arena games. They were most likely lowland gorillas or baboons, although Hanno described them as "wild women with hairy bodies."

But obscurity has always run hand in hand with our knowledge of apes, and what lay hidden in the Virungas remained a secret until the middle of the 19th century.

In the 1840s, scientists began to find large skulls that suggested there may still be an undiscovered great ape living in Africa. Consulting the Africans didn't clarify things; some thought there might be animals hiding in the mist-covered mountains, while others believed they were dangerous wild men, ostracized and alienated by their tribes.

And then in 1855, Paul Du Chaillu, a Franco-American explorer, traveled to Africa to find a mountain gorilla. His reports were loaded with hyperbole, filled with misleading information, and took years to dispel. For instance, he claimed because apes have yet to master fire, they often linger over smoldering, abandoned fires left by people—a fact we now know is not true.

He also promoted rumors that apes liked to kidnap human women, making wives of them after dragging them to their caves. These tales persisted through the years and made apes seem conniving and dangerous. Movies like *King Kong* (1933), starring Fay Wray, would help perpetuate the myth well into the 20th century.

But Du Chaillu is still credited as one of the first non-Africans to encounter mountain gorillas—and pygmies.

Edgar Rice Burroughs later immortalized him in his Tarzan series, where he based a character—Paul D'Arnot—on the mixed-race explorer. In *Tarzan of the Apes*, D'Arnot teaches Tarzan to speak English and French and prepares him for living amongst the civilized.

Three years after Du Chaillu´s expedition, in 1858, Charles Darwin and Alfred Wallace began publishing papers on what is now considered modern evolutionary thought, and the sudden discovery of these great apes—that seemed so similar to us— brought on much debate.

In 1902, a German explorer, Captain Oscar von Beringe, attempted to climb Mt. Sabyinyo—the mountain I was on—and encountered two mountain gorillas. He shot them and returned with their skins to Germany so scientists could study them, and soon after, they were assigned the name *Gorilla beringei beringei*.

And here I was, ninety-one years later, hoping to see a gorilla myself.

I had set out on a sunny day from the island of Lamu, off the coast of Kenya. The island was three hundred miles north of Zanzibar, where Sir Richard Burton and John Hanning Speke departed from on their quest to find the source of the Nile.

They had been following the Arab Slave Route, used by Muslim traders from Oman and Persia since 1825 to march newly captured slaves and ivory out of Africa, to Portuguese traders waiting on the coast.

In 1856 Burton and Speke left Zanzibar and pushed straight through Tanzania's savanna until nearly a thousand miles later, they came to the town of Ujiji, on the shores of Lake Tanganyika.

My journey would run parallel to theirs, ending in the Virunga Volcanic Range — located about 300 miles north of the lake.

First, I traveled by train and then in the back of pickup trucks where I hid from the rain under a tarp with the locals. Two weeks later, wet as a drowned rat, I had passed the Uganda-Zaire border crossing. At the time, it was a two-hut affair, run by one man on each side of the border.

From there I had walked a half day, led by a ten-year-old boy named Nick. He carried my backpack for a dollar into the foothills until we came to the gorilla base camp. It rained the entire time.

My traveling companion, a young English guy named James, had joined me in Uganda.

James and I had stayed the night in a simple hut, careful to avoid the many drips in the thatched ceilings. A smoldering fire did little to dry our clothes. When we set out the next morning, they were still damp — and now reeked of smoke.

We departed with two other tourists and two guides. One of the guides carried a big machete. He spent most of the time ahead of our small group scouting our way.

The other guide was named Rishi and had a rifle slung over his shoulder. He was now squatting next to me, silently waiting.

I glanced at his gun and asked, "Have you ever had to shoot a gorilla?"

Rishi solemnly stared at me and said, "I would shoot you before I shot a gorilla."

I held his stare, unsure if he was joking until his face cracked into a wide grin. He shrugged, "If necessary, I will use this gun for many things—but I would never shoot a gorilla with it."

A whistle blew from the direction I had last seen the other guide, and Rishi motioned for us to move again. We found the scout in a dense stand of bamboo a few minutes later. He pointed at the ground with the tip of his machete.

"A snare," said Rishi. He crouched to destroy it.

James asked, "Do many gorillas get killed by poachers?"

Rishi nodded. "Not just by poachers. Yesterday a whole troop was wiped out when they got in the middle of a crossfire between warring factions in Rwanda. The gorillas felt threatened and charged some of the soldiers, who cut them down with machine guns. It is a terrible thing."

The scout disappeared again, and we waited. I sank into my thoughts and remembered that the 1987 census estimated that only 254 gorillas were left in the Virungas.

Rishi coiled up the snare wire and stuck it in his small pack.

"Only two groups can visit the gorillas each day," he said. "We must keep their exposure to humans to a minimum."

James scratched his head. "If it's so important to keep exposure down, why are we here at all?"

Rishi nodded. "The money you give us pays for guards that keep poachers away. Without our efforts, there would be no gorillas left in the wild."

The scout returned, shaking his head, and we set off, following a steep, muddy track uphill.

A strong breeze greeted us when we reached a saddle that stretched between Mt. Sabyinyo and Mt. Bisoke. It ruffled my hair and momentarily cleared away the clouds and fog to give us an unobstructed view of the volcanic landscape. The yellow sunshine felt so good on my skin that I grinned while I surveyed the land.

The scope of the vista took my breath away. We could see almost all the peaks of this range, outlined in an emerald green swath that extended some twenty-five miles long. Potato crops and terraced fields extended from the base of the mountain and marked the national park's boundary.

From the saddle we looked down into western Zaire and Rwanda, and to Uganda in the northeast. Clouds still obscured the flanks of Mount Bisoke, but its volcanic peak thrust defiantly out of the mist.

Rishi nodded at the slope below us. "Down there is the domain of lions, leopards, and cheetahs, but they don't come up here. The tops of these mountains — from six to ten thousand feet — that is the territory of the gorillas."

Soon the mist gathered around us again and swallowed all sound.

How I wished I had my old gorilla photo with me now! On my last visit home, I'd searched for it unsuccessfully. But the image was etched deeply into my memory, and it seemed fresher in my mind with each step deeper into the Virungas.

The subject of that image was a mature male, somewhere between twenty and thirty years old. Mountain gorillas in the wild can live to forty. If the picture had been taken the year before I got it, in 1978, that gorilla could still be alive.

I wondered about the odds of seeing him.

A sharp whistle cut through the fog. It came from the bush on the Zaire side of the saddle and was our cue to follow.

Suddenly, the low rumble of thunder echoed up the mountainside, from Rwanda. Rishi paused, and his brow suddenly creased with wrinkles. It was raining yet again, as it had, off and on all day, and I wondered why another thunderstorm would bother him.

At least the rain temporarily washed the mud off.

Immersed in the primal jungle again, we followed a mucky buffalo track until we came upon the scout. He pointed at the ground where a palm and four great knuckles had created a perfect print in the mud.

We had just started to walk again when a loud crashing rose from the bush ahead of us and the ground shook. The scout motioned for us to squat down while Rishi unslung his rifle and fired two shots in the air.

The crashing stopped about forty feet away, and sudden silence swept over the jungle. The brush was so dense we couldn't see farther than a few feet.

Rishi listened cautiously, then turned to me and said, "Elephant."

A moment later, a low rumble shook the brush, and the beast began moving our way again. I scanned around in panic, wondering if I should flee.

Rishi fired three more rounds in the air, and we all waited nervously.

For a full minute there was no sound at all, then we heard the elephant moving away. Rishi sighed. "We will not see him again today."

"I think gorillas are close now," said Rishi in a whisper. I followed him deeper into a thicket of bamboo. The jungle steamed around us, and the world turned to shades of lime and emerald.

And then I glimpsed a shaggy, black head against the vibrant green.

I saw it only for a second before it disappeared, followed by a guttural bark.

But then, I glimpsed another one. At the edge of a clearing stood a mother gorilla with a young one clinging to her back.

She shyly looked at me, over her shoulder, before quickly retreating out of sight.

The scout followed, hacking a trail for us with his machete while making soft cooing sounds.

Soon we reached another small clearing in the bamboo where a group of eleven gorillas were munching on fresh shoots. We crouched in a circle and watched, about twenty feet away from them.

Scattered raindrops tapped the bamboo leaves above us and rustled the dead foliage beneath. The sun broke through, reflected off the innumerable drops turning the jungle into a magical kaleidoscope.

I counted four young gorillas. The rest were mature females.

One youngster—about two years old—crawled toward me, climbing over toppled bamboo. My heart pounded as the little gorilla came closer.

I recalled that females matured at about eight and gave birth to only one young every four years. At first, the infant clings to its mother, but it rides on her shoulders after around six months.

A musky, humanlike odor greeted me as the young gorilla plopped onto my lap.

I was thrilled that the young ape was interested in me. I stared into a set of eyes that seemed filled with curiosity, but then I realized he really wanted the red bandana I was wearing on my head.

He climbed up my torso—nearly making me pass out when I got a face full of his breath—and reached up for it.

Rishi noticed what was going on and said, "Do not let him take things."

I quickly took off the bandana and stuffed it in my pocket, and the little guy let out a wail.

Before I knew what was happening, a mother scurried up, grabbed the little gorilla, and disappeared into the bamboo. The others followed, and soon we were alone.

I knelt in the muddy undergrowth and watched the scout slowly follow the group of apes as they drifted away.

Rishi gestured for us to go, and I followed behind James.

While we crept through the jungle after Rishi, I thought about how curiosity is present in all primates, but especially in the great apes.

In the evolutionary history of primates, as monkeys and apes get more closely related to hominins, a more complex thought process, or cognition, develops.

Lemurs — among the most primitive primates — will investigate objects only as they would when foraging. If they can't eat it, they quickly lose interest. However, monkeys will readily manipulate objects until they determine if they might lead to food. A monkey will shake a rattle, but she will drop it once she realizes it produces nothing edible.

The great apes — chimpanzees, bonobos, gorillas and orangutans — are our closest living evolutionary relatives, and display behaviors strikingly similar to humans. They will not just investigate objects but also manipulate things that aren't edible, like when they are building nests.

All great apes are extremely curious. They explore their surroundings and are drawn to strange sounds or things that produce unexpected results. This contrasts with monkeys who soon grow bored with rattles, and never figure out that the reflection in the mirror isn't someone that needs to be watched.

And curiosity is the beginning of some incredible abilities: problem-solving, decision making, and a growing awareness of the self.

In humans, curiosity is a sign of intelligence and self-esteem, and there is a definite connection between curiosity and creativity.

I remembered the look of curiosity in the young gorilla's eyes.

The way he'd stared at me felt so familiar.

When George Schaller studied the mountain gorillas, he referred to the ape's manlike appearance, tremendous power, and intelligence as his "transcendent quality."

But I think Dian Fossey was more on the mark when she said, "Surely God, this is my kin."

We were on the move again, following the gorilla troop as they drifted deeper into the bamboo. Rishi gestured for us to proceed silently and to be careful not to make any quick movements.

After about ten minutes, the gorillas plunked down by an enormous hagenia tree with sprawling pads of moss draping the branches. They began feeding on some wild celery that grew at the base.

After their initial reluctance, the gorillas now seemed comfortable around us. Sprawled out on the wet grass, the little ones were rolling around excitedly, while the older females were munching away as they watched us.

And I could see that curiosity again in their eyes, watching us, not fearful, but careful, as a human mother would be around strangers. Was I anthropomorphizing again? Carl Akeley didn't anthropomorphize at all when he talked about gorillas. There was no touch of sentimentality when he wrote or spoke about them, yet he used words like "love" and "pity" to describe their actions.

I wondered just how self-aware these apes were.

Consciousness in animals is a tricky concept to define, even though it is clear that many creatures are conscious. All animals are aware to a certain point—they feel the weather, perceive pain, and are cognizant of what is happening currently around them.

Self-awareness is even more of a challenge to demonstrate, although a growing list of animals exhibit clear signs. Apes, dolphins, elephants, macaques, and even birds like crows and magpies have been proven to have measurable degrees of self-awareness.

The sun peeked through again, and I watched one of the older females lay back in the wet grass and point her face skyward to receive a few moments of sunshine. Just as a human would.

We had been told that direct eye contact with gorillas constitutes a threat, so I watched them with my peripherals.

James looked over at me, gave a thumbs-up as a female gorilla touched his head, and then sniffed his shirt. The gorilla looked him over, examining his clothing and the daypack he wore slung over his left shoulder.

He smiled deeply as he looked at her and said, "Well, hi there."

In Sumatra, I had also only encountered females and young among the orangutans, and I really wanted to see a mature male gorilla. I scanned the surrounding jungle and asked Rishi, "Where's the silverback?"

He replied in a low voice. "Oscar is the silverback for this group. He has been grumpy lately, so maybe it is better if he stays away."

It seemed more than a coincidence that the silverback was given the same name as the German explorer who shot the first gorillas on this very mountain in the name of science in 1902.

I caught a flicker of movement in the bamboo.

Something was lurking in the darkness, but the light was too dim to make out any details. I nodded that way to Rishi, who narrowed his eyes, stared for a moment, and then whistled to the scout.

When he had the man's attention, he gestured with his chin to the object I had seen. "That is him," he said.

A year-old male gorilla got bold and crawled over to James, scurried up his shoulder, and tried to pry his backpack off. I watched from my seat on a piece of fallen bamboo, about ten feet away.

The females watched us, chewing on fresh shoots. Aside from their chomping, the only other sounds were insects and the wind whispering over the top of the bamboo.

I felt like I had been dropped into one of Burrough's *Tarzan* stories. I'd waited for this experience all my life. Here I was, mesmerized, feeling like I had entered a world primitive and unspoiled.

Soon the young gorilla scrambled down from James' shoulder and approached me. He grabbed my hand and began sucking on my finger while looking up at me. I didn't know what to do.

The youngster noticed the tip of my red bandana sticking out of my pocket and grabbed it. I quickly took it back, and he shrieked in response.

I jolted and lost my balance. The bamboo stalk underneath me snapped loudly, and we both toppled backward.

I hadn't recovered from the tumble yet when I heard the galloping stride of something big approaching. I tried to spin around but was tangled up with the young ape, who continued to scream.

I knew what was coming was Oscar, the silverback. I heard him getting closer.

Then Oscar skidded to a stop right next to me.

Before I could blink, he thrust his face at mine, sniffing, his eyes penetrating and intense.

He glimpsed the young gorilla still squirming beneath me, and with a brush of his massive hand, knocked me away.

I lay there, head down in the wet foliage. Even though he couldn't see my face, I still squeezed my eyes shut because I was afraid of making him even angrier by staring.

I listened to him breathing for a moment, then opened my eyes slightly and stole a sideways look at him. He was standing next to me, not quite ready to let it go, and he kept glancing at me.

The youngster crawled over to me, and I sat up without looking at Oscar. The young ape was covered with dried leaves and seemed unfazed by our accident as he climbed on my hip. This seemed to calm the silverback somewhat.

With a thud Oscar sat down heavily beside me, and I admired him while he observed his family. His physical presence was magnificent: the massive chest, the flaring nostrils, his jet-black body sharply contrasting with the verdant jungle. The silverback had long fur, short but powerful arms, and broad hands and feet.

Twigs snapped under his weight as he settled.

I heard a rumble of thunder coming up from the south, in Rwanda, and Oscar turned his head that way and furrowed his brow. And then he looked back at me, most likely to reconfirm again that I wasn't a threat.

He placed one of his massive hands on my leg — it was the size of my head — and flopped me over. The little gorilla quickly hopped out of the way. I rolled with the movement and found myself on my back.

It was now difficult not to stare at him as he loomed over me.

I could see Rishi motioning for me to look away, but the way Oscar watched my every move had me captivated. His expression seemed strangely intimate. It felt familiar in the way that watching other humans is familiar. I sensed that he understood me in the same way.

In his piercing gaze, I thought I could hide nothing. This was no dog assessing if I was a danger, but a primate that understood my mind far better. I felt like I was staring back in time at one of my ancestors, to that prehistoric link that we both shared, to a deeply rooted connection.

After holding my eyes for a long moment, he looked away. He stared off at the bamboo, detached and majestic at once. I had the distinct feeling he was done with me. It was like some powerful tribal chief had dismissed me.

The youngster returned and tried to crawl on me again, but Oscar made a warning grunt, and we both froze. The silverback eyed me while scratching his armpit.

A moment later, the young gorilla moved away, and I breathed again.

We sat there for another ten minutes. I stole glance after glance at Oscar. The juxtaposition of his immensely powerful body and the calm, open face was stunning. And I was fascinated by the observant, penetrating eyes and the intelligence that lurked there.

When Rishi led us away, my mind was still spinning from that gorilla's gaze, as I knew it would over the days and months that followed.

That evening James and I returned to the damp hut and made plans to hike out of the Virunga range first thing in the morning. I was looking forward to dropping below ten-thousand-feet and escaping the cold air that chilled me to the bone. We hung our soggy clothes in front of the smoky woodstove once more, although I had little faith they would dry.

Below us, in Rwanda, I could hear the thunder again.

A hunched-over old lady scratched on the door and presented us with a steaming pot of potatoes and black beans. It had been a long day, with a lot of strenuous climbing and scrambling, and I was starved and dead-tired.

The food coursed nourishment through my body like an elixir, slowly returning my energy. When the old woman returned, I felt sociable again and asked her if another storm was coming.

She frowned and shook her head. "This is not thunder—it is shelling in Rwanda." I gave her a blank expression. Then I understood; she was referring to the civil war across the border.

At the time, I didn't know the difference between Tutsis and Hutus, or why they might hate each other, but I later learned that over the coming months, nearly one million people were slaughtered in that tiny country below us.

I thought about how Rishi had reacted when he had heard the thunder, and Oscar had also seemed disturbed by it.

Now I knew why.

During the last few days, the rumble of warfare had been in the air constantly. Apparently, only James and I had not known the cause of the thunder. The guards had been aware of it, and they knew it was a real possibility that one of the armies below might overrun them at any time. The gorillas were seeing the war as well, and in conjunction with poaching, were exposed to the atrocities of human violence almost every day.

The thought of it exhausted me, and soon after, I crawled into my sleeping bag.

Thanks to James and a couple of plastic trash bags, they were the only dry items we had. It was only 4:30 in the afternoon, but I didn't care as I slunk deeper into the bag.

How good it felt to be dry and warm.

Later, a storm did roll in. As I laid in my bag listening to it, I remembered the ape encounters I'd had and the magical mountain peaks around me. How strange to be in the place where Dian Fossey had worked and lived – and died brutally less than eight years before.

I had come to Zaire because it was currently the only country where one could see the gorillas. Because of Rwanda and Burundi's civil wars, nobody knew the fate of the mountain gorilla populations there.

I thought of the other volcanic peaks I had seen and wondered if there were any gorillas there at all.

I imaged my old gorilla photo and drifted off to sleep with the stern old ape watching over me.

Deep in the night, I woke from a nightmare in which I was in the movie theater in Panama again. "Gorillas in the Mist" was playing, and I watched in horror as the mob tore through the movie screen and right into the jungle, where they turned on the gorillas and killed them.

I sat up in the dark, disturbed, and lay awake until it was light enough to get dressed. It was time to leave the mountains.

The Virunga Volcanos, as seen
from Uganda. 1993.

The most dangerous of all apes, a human (*Homo sapiens*).
The author in Hwange National Park, Zimbabwe. 1993.

Chapter Seven

My tribe
(1993)

The walk back to the border post was downhill and slick. A foreboding ceiling of clouds hung just above us, drifting down, seemingly pursuing us. Like it might descend faster and try to block our retreat.

Behind us, the Virungas rumbled with thunder. At least I hoped it was thunder.

I thought of Oscar sitting there quietly.

Soon after we reached the border post, James located a pickup truck on the Ugandan side that was heading to Kabale.

There was room for four in the cab, but those seats had long been taken. We climbed in the back and waited an hour while the driver and his young assistant piled on goods and twenty-three more people. During that time, the light sprinkles I'd awakened to thickened into a heavier rain.

The driver unrolled a large, black plastic tarp and covered us. People on the edges of the truck bed tucked the tarp under their backsides and sat on it. Suddenly we huddled in the dark. The truck surged forward, and we shifted and leaned with the vehicle as if we were in a rugby scrum.

Pithecophilia

We were pressed tightly against each other, the sweet musky smell of humans filling my nostrils, their heavy breathing whispering in my ears. Twenty-five people huddled and in motion, like cigarettes in a discarded pack. I should have been claustrophobic, or maybe uncomfortable with such intimate contact with so many people—twenty-three Africans and a Brit—but it barely registered.

I bounced along with a detached stare, knowing I would not be dry until we reached Kampala, or maybe Nairobi. Knowing I was lucky for any ride I could find because only a fool travels in this area during the rainy season. And maybe I was being foolish—but I had communed with the gorillas. To me, that was worth any sacrifice.

When I later tried to recollect that day's journey, my mind flashed instead to the mountain gorillas lounging under the great hagenia tree, as if the humans that rode next to me were all of my troop—my tribe—and we were resting in the back of the truck, our nest, until it was time to move again.

I imagined us as apes. And as that idea spread through my mind, I saw all of mankind as apes—connected through our origins.

The driver navigated the mountain roads with a fearlessness that I could only hope was confidence. When the rain let up, he stopped and rolled up the tarp, but I found it was better not to see the precarious road. When we were under the tarp, the only thing to fear was my imagination.

Since descending the volcanos, I felt invincible, like Oscar had instilled in me some immunity to accidents.

Over the coming weeks, we took many different rides, and place names flashed by. At some of these locations, we rested and unsuccessfully tried to dry our clothes; others I glimpsed from under a banana-leaf umbrella as we passed.

Their names lingered in my mind. From the border town of Bunagna, we passed through Kisoro, Muko, Rubanda and Bubale—and that was to simply get back to Kabale, only thirty miles away. A washed-out road or flooded sections could turn ten miles into a full day journey.

And even though I was ready to leave rainy Uganda, I dragged my feet, taking side trips that often set us back a day or two. Some of these places I had yearned to see for years, like Jinja, the location of the source of the River Nile as it spills out of Lake Victoria.

And what an incredible feeling to watch as the waters of that mighty lake spill into a river—and know they will patiently flow for over four thousand miles before merging with the Mediterranean Sea.

In 1858 John Hanning Speke was euphoric when he stumbled upon Jinja and became the first European to set eyes on the lake. How I wished I could set the clock back two hundred years or so and beat him to it.

I contemplated shooting straight south, into Tanzania, to the town of Ujiri on Lake Tanganyika, where Stanley finally encountered Dr. Livingston. But in the end decided that venture was too far from Nairobi, where the rest of my gear waited in a locker.

Mostly James and I just learned to climb in, hold on, and white-knuckle it as we made our way back to Nairobi.

I remember one rainy day that seemed endless. I was dozing in the back of a truck, under a tarp, until a corner broke free and started flapping. It was a good thing because exhaust fumes were sneaking in through a hole in the bed, and I awoke feeling nauseous.

When we stopped an hour later for gas, James limped around to get some feeling back into his numb left leg that a large woman had sat on for two hours. We split a coke and ate some barbequed goat silently while we waited for the loading to begin again.

There was no point in complaining.

And James had a great disposition, which helped. I can still hear him saying, "Oh, lovely, they have goat."

Before long, the Ruwenzori Mountains rose ahead of us, and then were swallowed silently by gray storm clouds. When we stopped near Fort Portal, I peeked out from under the tarp to see at least twenty Marabou storks staring down at me from the tree under which we were parked.

Occasionally I spotted other white people, but I never felt uncomfortable amid the sea of black faces that always surrounded me. They were open and friendly as they greeted me from the doorways of shelters or dry porches, or as they climbed into a vehicle by my side.

I still felt the gloomy shadow of the war in Rwanda looming over me, but I shook it over time and began to feel how these people looked — relaxed.

Strangely, the experience of sitting with the gorillas had changed how I felt towards my fellow man. I blindly trusted my travel companions. I had little for others to steal, the few notes I had hidden in the lining of my belt, but I wouldn't have cared if even that disappeared.

When I had food, I shared it with those near me. And as I handed it out, I again flashed back to watching the apes peacefully feeding and playing. I tried to make room for others, even when the space was tight. I wanted to interact with my fellow man with that same harmonious sentiment that I experienced in the Virungas.

I wondered if I was applying animal characteristics now to humans, instead of the other way around. The opposite of anthropomorphizing is called dehumanization, but that didn't fit here. Dehumanization is defined as "treating other people as if they lack human capacities and are not worthy of equality."

But I found it the opposite. If I said the humans were acting like apes, it was a compliment. I remembered the orangutans that had surrounded me when I was lost in Sumatra's Gunung Leuser National Park. The concern that I thought I had seen in the older female's eyes had relaxed me. I wasn't scared.

As we got closer to Kampala, the pickup trucks became a rarer means of transportation, and we found ourselves traveling more by matatus. These were minibusses with padded benches bolted to the floor and carried about twenty people. Out of the rain now, I sang along to the crazy beat of a popular local song with the other passengers and shared my supply of peanut bars.

When we finally reached Nairobi, I said goodbye to James.

But I didn't fly back to America.

Instead, I purchased a flight to South Africa and made plans to hitchhike my way back—nearly two-and-a-half-thousand miles—to catch my original flight, which I'd postponed for three more months.

There is an African proverb that states, "Once you have drunk of Africa's waters, you will drink again," and I was still thirsty.

I sojourned a few weeks in Nairobi, obtaining visas and assembling other supplies until my departure date. During that time, I submitted several articles to a newspaper called *The Nation*. While researching one of the stories on a Maasai dance group, I was befriended by several of the dancers who invited me to their apartment.

Several times, I stopped by after their practice to visit and hang out for a while. They seemed as curious about my world as I was about theirs. In one of our conversations, a young man asked what nicknames I had when I was young.

I thought of how the middle school kids had changed DeMayo into DeMayonaise—thanks to Louis Gossett Jr. in the movie *An Officer and a Gentleman*—and taunted me endlessly. Later, that evolved into Miracle Whip, and then just Whip.

I spared him that story and told him that one of my nicknames was Whip. He grinned and said, "Then, you are Kiboko."

It turns out Kiboko is a Swahili word for both the hippo, and a whip made from a hippo's hide.

I grew an affinity for hippos after that and found myself drawn to them almost as much as I was to primates. And on future journeys to Africa, I often introduced myself as Kiboko, which turned out to be a great way to break the ice.

Through the coming years I couldn't get enough of Africa. On four trips to east and southern Africa, I covered over ten thousand miles on overland journeys.

I was in my twenties, an adrenaline junkie, and I could claim it was because of all the beckoning adventures: My first time in a climbing harness, I completed a multi-pitch ascent of the 17,057-

foot Mount Kenya. A few months later, I descended to the bottom of the deepest gold mine in South Africa - 7,800 feet below the earth´s surface.

But the truth is it was something more. Something deeper.

Since my encounter with Oscar, I had been trying to understand just what I had seen in his stare. I felt I had witnessed both something familiar and something alien.

In the long eons since man—*homo sapiens*—separated from apes, our minds evolved differently. Hominization, or the process of becoming human, took place over millions of years, and no one is absolutely certain what led to the development of our remarkable cognitive capacities. We do know now that individuals don't evolve, populations do, and that there is something unique in what we became.

It can still be easily argued that apes are self-aware, but clearly not as highly evolved as humans. The most studied member of the ape family are chimpanzees. There is plenty of evidence of self-recognition with them, using the forehead dot test. But even then, up to 40% of the chimps tested did not recognize themselves in the mirror.

I began to think I was looking at this from the wrong perspective—maybe self-awareness wasn't what I was searching for in apes.

In humans, the part of our mind that is active when you think about yourself is called the default mode network. It is the source of the running narrative in your head. This is where your ego resides. When you think about your past, your future, or any opinion you might have, your thoughts are bouncing around in your default mind.

This part of the brain hasn't evolved in the same way in apes as in humans. Bear with me for a moment, as I am not saying that apes don't have intellect, personalities or emotions—they clearly do. It's just that their brains are wired differently.

In the Sixties and Seventies, a vast amount of research was conducted on human subjects that ingested psilocybin, found in psychedelic mushrooms, and then observed during therapeutic experiments. Through this data and ongoing research, we now know that psilocybin has the potential to boot you out of your default brain network.

When I read this, I had an aha-moment.

A few years earlier, when I was obsessed with freeing that gibbon I called Papillon in Thailand, I had a strange experience.

After I had healed from my motorcycle accident, I ate some psychedelic mushrooms with my Mexican friend, Franco. For about four hours, I could not remember my name, the country I was from, or the country I was in. I found it all hysterically funny, but not a problem.

For years after, I wondered why I could not produce an answer to a question that I would have thought was so core to my being — my name. Honestly, I couldn't fathom why I couldn't answer it.

Now I understood why: the psilocybin had knocked me out of my default brain — the part of my mind where the "I" resided.

The more I thought about it, the more it seemed like when I was in that state, I may have been closest to understanding one aspect of how an ape's mind might work.

In one sense, the experience had been pretty normal. I was sitting there quietly, enjoying the island breeze, watching the waves break on the beach. I took everything in so directly that my mind never wandered.

I was in the moment, unconcerned with the past or the future — in fact, they were mostly inaccessible. I felt connected to nature.

And I felt a love for everything around me. The negative faded away, and I didn't dwell on things unless they pinged my curiosity.

I felt primal and primitive.

Clearly, this is my pithecophilia kicking in.

Among all the animals on this planet, we — humans — are alone in being able to contemplate our place on it over time. This is a change in awareness that we alone underwent in the long years since we separated from apes, our closest living relatives, and the most significant difference in how our minds work.

We know this by studying archaic man, who believed himself to belong to the ecosystems he lived in, but also created art and held funerals for the dead.

Both things require an understanding of the world and your place in it. And for early man, art wasn't just an occasional occupation, but a core way in which he explained his world. To do this, you need the default brain, the "I."

The more I thought of it, the more I reflected on the creation myth of Adam and Eve, as depicted by the Abrahamic religions. In the story, Adam and Eve are told they can eat freely from any fruit in the garden except the tree that contained "the knowledge of good and evil."

As we all know, Eve ate from the tree, and then Adam did, and after that, they were banished from the Garden of Eden.

I always believed that story was about the moment when man — *homo sapien* or some earlier hominin — looked around and realized he was different from the other animals. He realized he would die, and by that point, he had a consciousness that allowed him to think about it.

Could it be that the story of Adam and Eve was really about the consequences of developing the default brain network? After all, once you realize that you exist outside of nature, you can't go back.

In a sense, you are banned from the Garden.

And when I was tripping on mushrooms, I felt I was allowed back into the Garden — maybe because I had lost the ability to contemplate the difference between good and evil. The flow of information in my mind seemed to run on images, not words.

Does that somehow make Oscar a modern-day Adam? In my book it does.

I thought of how he had looked at me in the cool bamboo forest. The gorilla had taken one long stare and then turned away. I felt like he was "done with me" and I was starting to understand why.

While Oscar looked me over, I am sure his sapient mind compared me to a few other humans he'd encountered. He looked me in the eye, the way a human would, too.

But at the same time, he took in my scent, and my pheromones had told him much more. Without a second glance, he could tell if I was afraid, or maybe hiding something, and I had passed that test.

So, when he looked away, he had no doubt concluded that I wasn't a threat—based on his real-life experience. And he didn't have the type of brain that let him become paranoid and keep second-guessing that fact—unless circumstances changed, he *was* done with me.

A few months later, I was traveling independently, making my way from South Africa through Zimbabwe to Zambia. My plan was to flag down an overland truck heading north from Lusaka, and eventually return to Nairobi for my flight back to the states.

While camping at the Great Zimbabwe ruins near Masvingo, I came across a tattered novel called *Altered States* by Paddy Chayefsky. There was a movie adaptation of it in 1980 starring William Hurt.

After reading it, I was almost fearful of my mysterious hidden ape brain.

The plot follows Edward Jessup, a psychopathologist studying schizophrenia during the seventies. Jessup believes we contain "other states of consciousness that are as real as our waking states" and uses an isolation tank and a cocktail of psychoactive drugs to uproot them. The novel is actually based on sensory deprivation research conducted by John C. Lilly while on mescaline and LSD.

And for a while I thought Jessup might have been on to something. It initially sounded like Carl Jung's quest to find the "two-million-year-old ape within each of us."

Jung was a Swiss psychoanalyst who believed we modern humans inherited a collection of ancestral experiences that combined in our minds to form archetypes. Thus, we all know the trickster or the hero.

And like Edward Jessup, Jung thought the secrets of our ancestral brains could be found through combining mescaline and psilocybin mushrooms with shamanic traditions.

The research of the fictional character Jessup of course takes a scary turn when he emerges from the floatation tank as a feral hominin — a six-million-year-old *Sahelanthropus* — who goes on a rampage through the city until passing out in a zoo.

I thought of my family and friends finding me naked in a zoo, covered with antelope blood, and shuddered. As much as I wanted to understand apes, even I had my limits.

I had no desire at this time to turn into an earlier version of my evolutionary self.

One bright morning I searched for a bus leaving Bulawayo for Victoria Falls. I found one parked in the shade. A white-haired old man with a patched eye sold me a ticket and then walked away.

I boarded the bus and headed down the aisle. It was not a matatu, but a full-sized school bus. Most of the seats were taken, so I shuffled to the back, holding my backpack over my head.

Soon others began boarding, and at first, everyone sat there quietly watching the other buses out the narrow windows. The driver still called for more people to board, and before long, the crowd of people grew so thick that even the folks with seats stood.

I got up as well. If I hadn't, a dozen men would have pushed back to sit on my lap. Luckily, it was a cool morning, and even though the windows only opened a few inches, it was enough to allow a sweet breeze to blow over our heads – about a foot below the roof of the bus.

The passengers were mostly women, and older men, with a few children tucked in as well, and despite the tight quarters, there seemed to be a pleasant vibe in the air.

The driver let a few more people squeeze through the door before he closed it, and then fired up the engine. Next to me stood an older woman with a thin red scarf wrapped over her head. She politely smiled at me, and I said, "I don't know if I can make it like this all the way to Vic Falls."

The woman, whose face was only inches away, shook her head and said, "This bus does not go that way. We are heading east — in the other direction."

We both began calling to the bus driver, but he couldn't hear us. Some passengers in the middle of the bus asked the woman what was happening, and she explained in Shona.

Soon, word was sent from person to person until the driver was notified, and he shut down the engine. He got up and looked at me, from thirty feet away, over the heads of a hundred or more people.

"Where do you go?" he asked.

"Victoria Falls," I replied, and he sighed and shook his head.

"Come," he finally said with a hand gesture.

I had been peering at him through the gap between the ceiling and the coarse black hair of a hundred people. But when I suddenly lowered my gaze, I saw a dense collage of faces staring at me blankly, waiting to see what I would do.

I glanced sideways and could quickly discern that there was no way I could squeeze out one of the windows, and the bus was packed way too tightly for me to wiggle my way through.

I realized it would take an hour to unload and load the passengers again: I was sure the driver didn't want to do that. I shrugged my shoulders — a gesture he couldn't see — and asked, "How?"

A hundred sets of white eyes shifted from me to the driver.

Now, realizing this could make him late, he held up both hands and made the same gesture, but more urgently, "Come! Come!"

In front of me, a sea of shining white teeth flashed, and then as many hands made the same gesture.

I handed up my backpack and watched it float over a collage of hands, surfing toward the front, until the driver grabbed and set it by his feet.

Then he motioned for me to come.

I weighed close to two hundred pounds, and the people around me were a pretty mixed crowd in terms of strength.

Still, the driver urged me forward.

The people next to me helped me begin my journey to the front of the bus by holding out two sets of interlaced fingers, and before long, I found myself moving over the crowd, crawling over their heads.

I was careful not to kick anyone. When I slowly moved a leg forward, hands would appear that supported the knee, and others gripped my feet so I could put pressure on them. I sensed that the crowd ensured that others lent their hands if one individual had too much weight to carry.

It was like a gentle, slow-motion mosh pit.

My face passed within inches of the faces of the people supporting me, and each took the opportunity to make eye contact.

"Hallo," a few said in English, but most spoke words I didn't know.

They were probably addressing me in Shona, but it also could have been Chewa, Khoisan, Ndebele, Sotho, Xhosa, or a dozen other languages spoken in Zimbabwe.

They whispered at me, phrases I couldn't understand, but the friendly message in their eyes warmed me, and I nodded back. But how I wished I could say just a few words in their languages.

Not understanding the people around you is common when traveling. Not only do you often not know their language, but many times the situation and cultural circumstances leave you entirely uninformed.

For this reason, I always tried to speak the truth when I was on the road—even if it might put me in danger. Make the few words I uttered, be honest. I never lied about being American or what my beliefs were. I always felt truthfulness in speech is the basis for being honest with yourself.

And if you lie, most people can smell it anyway. So, speak truthfully.

I yearned to converse with the other passengers as I slowly crawled over them. And as my eyes swept from face to face, I thought of the mountain gorillas again, who converse for the most part without words but in a way that expresses their desires with facial expressions and body language.

I smiled — and realized that said everything I wanted to express.

Suddenly, everyone below me began smiling back.

I laughed, and laughter bubbled back at me.

I found it strange to feel so loved in that crowded bus. Like I was with the apes again. A wave of emotions passed through me with the thought, "My tribe."

The last of my money was hidden in the lining of my belt, and my passport in a holder held tightly to my chest, but I had little fear of being robbed.

Nothing would have surprised me more as I crawled along.

And in that way, I crept through that little space, over the heads of a hundred people. And by the time I got off the bus, I almost regretted not taking the ride with my new friends.

When the bus finally pulled away, they were all waving and shouting goodbye. The sight of their hands sticking out the windows filled me with joy. I knew those hands.

Over the years, incidents like this helped shape my world view, from self-preservation to a global love of humanity — my fellow humans.

We are one tribe. To believe or live anything else is to retreat into the shadows. It's this damn default brain that gets us into trouble. We think too much about ourselves — our personal priorities. And not about others or how we can be helpful to others.

We think too much — and not about the things that truly matter.

Pithecophilia

Robert Louis DeMayo

Book Two

1994 - 2010

Rhesus Macaque (*Macaca mulatta*).
Habitat: Grassland and forest areas. Range: South, Central and SE Asia.

Chapter Eight

Hanuman
(1994)

*T*he mournful call of a peacock roused me from a dream—a dream in which a tiger had been growling. I lay in bed, tucked under a mosquito net, and watched the world awaken outside my open window.

For a decade, I had traveled for six months each year, always making sure I skipped the entirety of the New England winter. These travels took me to every continent except Antarctica.

This lifestyle kept me on the move and never really allowed me to put down roots; I was always either traveling, working non-stop and getting ready to travel, or crash-landing at home, skinny and broke.

I don't think anyone was more surprised than me when, at twenty-nine, I ended up with a girlfriend who could keep up with me.

I was still beset with a bad case of Pithecophilia, and hardly knew what I wanted to do with my life other than travel, but that didn't seem to bother her.

Dee was from Maine, a few years younger than me, and on her way to California when I hijacked her life and fell in love with her.

We dated for two months before moving in together for a month, then traveled around Asia for half a year.

She appeared to love the road as much as I did. With her by my side, the world felt like a fuller place. My travel highlights began to revolve around showing her things.

We started with a trip to southeast Asia, where we rock climbed the fabulous limestone cliffs of Thailand's Krabi area, explored the Mekong River as it cut through Laos, and then moved on to a lengthy trek into Nepal's Annapurna range.

I looked over at her sleeping form and thought about how badly that trek had turned out. She lay there, pale, dark circles around her eyes, sleeping like the dead.

From our starting point outside Pokhara, in western Nepal, the trek stretched 160 miles as it completely circled the Annapurna Range. It was late spring, but maybe not late enough. Travelers we met on the trail informed us that the pass in the middle of the trek — Thorung La pass at 17,769 feet — was closed due to recent snow. But we pushed on anyway, hoping someone would blaze their way through before we got there.

The trail followed a river, passing small villages built of stone and multi-leveled verdant rice paddies. When we first set out, we were so low in the foothills that we couldn't even see the peaks.

Dee skipped along, slowing to spin every prayer wheel she passed when we entered or left a village. For the first few days, we hiked ten miles a day. The weather was glorious, and I barely noticed the foreboding clouds that hovered around the higher peaks when they came into view.

We were on the backside of the Annapurna Range, and as we gained elevation, we glimpsed mountains to our northeast in Tibet. Most of the villages on this side of the range were populated by Tibetans who had come from there.

Those distant summits were soon dwarfed by the Annapurnas, a range with fourteen peaks that stretch more than twenty-three thousand feet into the cobalt blue sky. The highest, Annapurna I, sits at 26,545 feet. In 1950 a French expedition led by Maurice Herzog summitted it via the north face.

I felt light-headed with the dazzling brilliance of the snow-covered summits.

But over the next sixty miles, we slowly ran out of steam.

It began to rain every afternoon, and more than once, we got caught by a storm just before we reached a village with shelter. As we gained altitude, the cold drizzle seemed to sink deeper into our bones.

Finally, we found ourselves stuck in a tiny village with too many other stranded travelers. The wind whistled through the stone houses, and the cold bore down on us like a cider press. A sickness swept through the village, and we got it.

We turned around, short of the pass, and tried to hightail it out the way we had come in, but it was too late. Dysentery and a stomach bug meant that we could barely walk five hundred steps without having to pull our pants down or throw up.

But there was no other option. The only airport in the area was on the other side of the pass, unreachable now, and the nearest road was at the beginning of the trail where we were now heading back to.

Dee developed a fever and became delirious, and we had to stop forty miles from the trailhead. We had no medicine, but another traveler gave me some Tylenol, which helped.

After about forty-eight hours the fever broke, and I rented a donkey to carry her out the remaining miles. Often the burro wouldn't move unless I pulled him forward with my full weight. It was terribly slow going. We trudged along in a daze.

Another traveler gave me some tiniba—an antibiotic used to treat bacterial or parasitic infections—and slowly, we got our bowels under control.

But Dee was still delirious, and I hardly felt in control of myself enough to be responsible for her. One morning, I almost lost her over the side of a suspension bridge when the donkey jumped over a missing plank.

The pounds fell off us. By the time we reached the paved road, I had lost a quarter of my body weight. Dee was ghostly and emaciated.

Pithecophilia

We stumbled into Pokhara after three weeks in the mountains.

There, we visited a Tibetan doctor who practiced an ancient medicinal tradition called Sowa-Rigpa. The experience was somewhat mystical, with incense burning in the corner of the room, and nobody speaking a word of English while he took our pulses at three different locations.

He had two assistants, who also took our pulses, and then nodded at the doctor in assent. As sick and weak as I was, I clung to that gesture as hope that we might be cured. The sore muscles and blisters from the long miles hurt, but what was worse was the unknown sickness that inhabited our bodies, leaving us both achy.

He gave us instructions—through gestures—that we couldn't consume certain foods: no dairy, no sugar, no fried or greasy foods. And we were to eat some small black pellets dissolved into hot tea several times a day.

They looked like goat turds, and they tasted like what I imaged a goat turd would taste like, too.

Other than that, he gave no explanation of our illness.

But beginning that evening, we drank our tea as ordered. We honored the food restrictions, too.

Almost instantly, we both began to feel better.

We stayed that night in Pokhara, and the next evening we took an overnight bus to Bharatpur, located in Nepal's subtropical lowlands—an area known as the Terai.

Here the Himalayan foothills merge onto the Indo-Gangetic Plain and form tall grassland and scrub savannas. In 1973 a large portion of the area was set aside as Chitwan National Park. It was made a World Heritage Site in 1984.

Until the middle of the 19th century, this area had been almost inaccessible for humans, and the bigger mammals like tigers and rhinoceros thrived. For centuries it was known as the Heart of the Jungle.

We had arrived the day before, traumatized by the numerous near-miss accidents on the insane overnight bus ride. It seems to me that most south Asian bus drivers crave death — or maybe it's rebirth.

But before we could relax, we had to take another local bus to a small village located next to the national park.

Around noon we checked into a guest house on a ridge that looked down at the Rapti River. Chitwan was about a half-mile away, on the other side of the stream, but because of the noonday glare, I didn't even glance that way.

We got a room on the second floor and limped up the stairs.

Dee and I collapsed on the bed, opened our eyes two hours later, just long enough to shower and change into something clean, then sunk back to sleep like we had been drugged.

Outside my window the sky was growing lighter, and Dee stirred next to me.

It was hot. Even before the sun broke the horizon, the day was warmer than any we had experienced in the mountains. I felt like one of those frozen frogs that slowly thawed back to life when spring finally arrives.

The peacock cried out again and was answered by another bird.

Suddenly I glimpsed movement in the corner of the window.

Cautiously, a small hand reached into our room and felt along the windowsill. Thief! My mind screamed.

I quickly reached under my pillow, where I had stashed my money belt the night before — and was relieved to find it.

All that was vulnerable to theft was a half-bunch of bananas I had bought at the bus station the day before, and my jackknife.

I sat up, and then noticed that the hand was incredibly small, with long fingers. And as it reached for the bananas, I realized it belonged to a primate.

The hairy forearm confirmed my guess, and when the little fella poked its head up to scan my room, I realized it was a Rhesus Macaque (*Macaca mulatta*).

While it held my stare, its hand slowly moved to the bananas.

Rhesus monkeys are brown or grey with a tail of eight or nine inches. They don't get much heavier than seventeen pounds.

This one was light brown, looked about twelve pounds, and although I am hardly an expert on macaques, I guessed it was a female.

She had a small pink face that was free of fur, and I thought there was something feminine about her.

There were only a few bananas left in the bunch, and I didn't mind if she took them, so I smiled and addressed her.

"Enjoy your brekkie," I whispered as I watched the fruit quietly slip out the window.

A few moments later, the hand reappeared, this time edging its way toward my jackknife — which I did not want to be stolen.

I slipped past the mosquito net and jumped out of bed, but I had forgotten that my feet were still swollen and blistered, and my muscles sore and knotted — with some fresh damage from the bus ride.

I collapsed to the floor with a thump, instantly scaring off my simian visitor and waking Dee.

Two hours later we were dressed and were slowly limping our way down the dusty road. We had showered and then addressed our injuries before leaving. Our feet were still covered with wounds, our shoulders rubbed raw from the pack straps, and Dee had saddle sores from riding the burro.

In Pokhara, we had purchased bandaids and antiseptic cream, and as we slowly shuffled to breakfast, my cuts and blisters screamed under the white-hot pain of the sanitizer.

It had been cold in the mountains, and often we had walked on a layer of snow, but now we were back in the heat. From Pisang, at twelve thousand feet of elevation, to Chitwan, we had dropped more than ten thousand feet.

It was still morning, but it had to be at least ninety degrees already. Even with sunglasses on, I could barely see because of the glare.

A short walk along the dirt road led to several small, family-run restaurants, but as we trudged along, they seemed to be miles away, and the sun singed me as if I were a bug under a magnifying glass.

"How about that place?" suggested Dee, hopefully, as we approached the first restaurant.

A sign read: New Nepali Friendly Café. "Sounds perfect."

The structure was dust-covered and plain from the street, but when we stepped inside, cool shadows enveloped us. There were a few tables clustered near the door, but most of the seating was in an open courtyard where a half-dozen tables were set in the shade of a grove of palms.

Strings of small lights were strung around the courtyard's perimeter, and I got the impression that the location might double as a disco at night.

In the distance beyond the courtyard, the land was sculpted by terraced fields that fell away until they reached the river; on the other side, an immense grassland extended to a wall of jungle shimmering in the haze, a few miles away.

I took off my sunglasses, hung my daypack over the back of a chair, and plopped down at one of the tables in the courtyard.

Instantly I felt a hundred sets of eyes on me.

It took a moment for my own vision to adjust, but when I looked around, I could see that a large troop of rhesus macaques had taken over the far end of the courtyard. There was a small lawn visible beyond the courtyard, and most of them were gathered there. But a dozen or so had encroached on the restaurant and were raiding the sugar packets on one of the far tables.

The macaques acted like they owned the place. Some chased each other and played, others groomed their young—and on the lawn, a few were sleeping.

In the kitchen, an old man and several younger women— daughters or granddaughters from the look of it—chatted excitedly about this predicament.

"You will have no trouble if you stay in your seats," said a young Nepali man wearing a khaki shirt who was seated at a table next to us.

He looked about twenty. He had a topographical map open in front of him, and a pair of binoculars lay on it.

Dee glanced over at the monkeys apprehensively, and the man added with a smile, "Of course, you may want to wait a while before ordering your food, or they will steal it."

The older man came out of the kitchen with a broom and chased the monkeys off the table and on to the lawn, but when he pushed them further, they bared their teeth and refused to give more ground.

Resigned, the man grabbed a tray and cleared the spices and condiments off the outer tables, then retreated into the kitchen.

A few minutes later, a young woman slowly walked our way to take our order. She looked to be in her late teens and had a casual, relaxed look on her face, but never in my life have I seen someone who could walk so unhurried. It seemed to take an eternity for her to cross the room.

Over the coming days I would joke about her and her super-human way of decelerating time. I nick-named her Speedy.

At the table next to us, the young Nepali man caught my eye and introduced himself just as the waitress finally arrived.

"Hi," he said, "my name is Veeren."

The waitress raised her hand to her mouth to cover a giggle.

Veeren glared at her, and then returned his focus to us. "Have you considered a guided walk into the national park?"

In our current state the idea of a hike seemed comical.

"Not yet," I said, and then turned to the waitress, "but we could use two cups of hot tea."

She nodded her head, almost imperceptibly, and then turned away.

Dee gave an involuntary shiver at the idea of the tea, which indeed was improving our health, but still tasted horrid once the goat turd-like pellets dissolved into it.

"You must visit the grasslands," continued Veeren, "we would cross the river just there," he said, pointing at the Rapti River far below, where I could now see on the far bank a small structure and several men. He handed his binoculars to Dee so she could see it better.

"I will get the paperwork beforehand—you need a permit to enter the national park. On my morning walks, I see so many animals. Sloth bears, rhinos, deer and monkeys, and you may even glimpse a tiger!"

The waitress—still only a few paces away on her long journey back to the kitchen—suffered from another fit of giggles at this comment, and Veeren's eyes bored a hole in her back.

He shook it off and glanced at the macaques as two skirmishing males knocked over a chair. He chuckled. "But who wants to go on safari when you can see so many animals right here in town?"

"Is it always this bad?" I asked.

"No," he answered. "Men used to trap them in the cities and export them for scientific use, but since 1977 that has been banned. In the wild, you rarely see them in groups of more than seventy, but I've heard now in big cities like Jaipur and Delhi they roam in mobs of six or seven hundred."

I knew a little about rhesus macaques: They are considered generalists and thus incredibly successful in adapting to various habitats, including mountains, forests, and grasslands, but also occur close to human settlements. They have the widest geographic distribution of all non-human primates, with a range that extends through Southern, Central, and Southeastern-most Asia.

The International Union for Conservation of Nature, established in 1964 to track the endangerment of Earth's species, lists them as "least concern."

That seemed a little harsh to me. I know there are a lot of them and the rating simply means they're not endangered, but "least concern" seems a bit mean considering how many have died at the hands of scientists for research. For years they were considered the primate of choice; even into this century, up to seventy thousand macaques suffer, yearly, in laboratories in the name of science.

They were the first primate to be cloned in 1999, and the first primate to have its genome sequenced in 2006.

In 1959, a rhesus macaque became the first primate to be shot into space in a rocket and survive. Nobody talks about the ones that died.

They should be heroes for their unconsenting sacrifices.

A large male macaque ambled toward the kitchen. When he peered in the door, shouting ensued, and then a pan came flying out.

The macaque retreated hastily to the lawn.

"What can you do about it?" Dee asked.

Veeren gave a shy grin and said, "In some parts of India, they use langurs to keep them at bay. There's supposedly a man in this village with a tame langur that he rents out by the day — but I've yet to see him."

Dee gave him a blank stare, and he added, "Langurs are another type of monkey we have here. Men go into the forest and trap them; then, they are tamed, so they live with the farmers as pets. The males can grow to forty pounds, so they are bigger than the macaques and can scare them off."

"Doesn't the Forest Department have a problem with that?" I asked.

Veeren nodded his head. "Certainly, but they are understaffed, and their efforts to get on top of the macaque problem by trapping them and releasing them deep in the forest doesn't seem to work at all — they simply come back."

We all looked at the monkeys for a while, watching them frolic.

"The problem is, the forests are disappearing, and the macaques have learned to eat what we eat. They even know to look through windows and see what we have that might be accessible."

"We're becoming their food source," said Dee.

He scanned the troop, sprawled out on the lawn and said, "I guess we're lucky they're not maneaters."

I chuckled at his jest.

I asked, "Are there maneaters here?"

He bobbled his head slightly and said, "But, of course. You can get maneaters wherever there are tigers. These cats will eat people when certain conditions arise."

"Like what?" asked Dee.

"Most tigers that attack humans do so out of desperation," said Veeren. "The Thak man-eater was a tigress, killed by Jim Corbett, who ate four men. Corbett noted that she had two old gunshot wounds, and one had become septic. The Tiger of Segur killed five people in the 1950s, and it was later discovered he had a disability that prevented him from hunting his natural prey."

Dee kept scanning the savanna with the binoculars as if even from this great distance, she might spot a tiger lurking there.

I caught Veeren's eye and said, "I noticed you said 'most'."

He sighed. "Unfortunately, some of the most successful man-eaters had nothing wrong with them. It is estimated that over the last five centuries, over one million people have been eaten by tigers — more than by any other big cat."

I remembered the story of The Ghost and The Darkness, two famous man-eating lions that killed and consumed 135 men — mostly Indian railway workers — in what is now Kenya's Tsavo National Park. When I asked if India or Nepal had equally notorious cats, he told me about the Champawat Tiger.

He seemed to tense up. His eyes never left the grasslands while he spoke. "This tigress killed two hundred people here in Nepal before she was driven away — and then she went on to kill another 236 men and women in India."

I found myself reliving the moments in the Sumatran jungle when I had been lost, and the ever-present fear of a tiger sneaking up on me that persisted into the evening.

Veeren seemed to be talking to himself when he added, "She was fearless. They say she would enter a village in broad daylight and roar until someone would panic and flee their hut."

Dee gulped and said, "How terrifying it must have been."

We sat there for a moment to let that horrid vision settle. Veeren looked agitated, and his eyes kept sweeping the distant savanna.

When we stood to leave, he observed us slowly limping toward the door and said, "When you are fit, we will go into the national park."

I nodded. "One step at a time."

Over the coming week we saw Veeren several times, usually in the morning when we drank our first cup of goat turd tea. When he had clients to guide, they set out before sunrise and tried to be back by ten—about when we arrived for breakfast.

When he had no clients, he would come by for a late breakfast and then disappeared before the heat of the day set in.

We learned that he had just recently obtained his guiding license, and when he told stories of his animal encounters, there was an excitement—a freshness—that made me yearn to go with him as soon as we were able.

He knew of our aversion to the tea and teased me, nodding his head at my cup while chiding, "You must drink your medicine—it will only taste worse cold."

Once I tried adding sugar to the tea, and within a few sips, my belly began to gurgle. On another day, Dee added just a splash of milk, and right away, spit it out. After that, we didn't break the rules.

At night, I dreamt of fried food.

But we continued to heal. I guess it didn't matter that we did not know what sickness we had had or what was contained in the medicine the Tibetan doctor gave us. It worked.

We slept. We walked. We ate. We slept.

The hot season was upon us, and like Veeren, we often retreated to our room before noon, and only came out in the evening, after the cool evening enveloped the village.

Truth be told, it was usually hunger that drove us from the room.

But we were getting acclimated, and it wasn't as big a shock to the system as it was when we first arrived.

I always hoped I would bump into Veeren when we came out for the night. But I never saw him after the sun went down.

One sunny morning I sat at the New Nepali Friendly Café, observing Speedy barreling towards me in slow motion with a plate of scrambled eggs and some sliced avocado. We had finished our prescribed week of tea drinking and could now eat normally.

A dozen macaques were visiting the courtyard. A few were scampering in the palms above us, causing a pair of kingfishers to squawk in complaint.

As Speedy slowly closed the distance, I imagined how good the food would taste. My mouth watered, and I watched her like a predator, waiting for her to get just a little bit closer before I pounced.

Veeren entered the courtyard. I gestured at one of the chairs at our table, and he sat down across from Dee and me.

He wore a big grin. "I saw you walking yesterday — you are getting stronger! Maybe now you want to go into the park?"

Dee sipped her coffee and said, "There was such a beautiful sunset last night — could we go at the end of the day?"

Veeren´s voice became deadpan as he said, "No. If you want to go on a night drive, your guesthouse can arrange it with one of the companies. I only do walking tours in the morning."

He leaned back, out of the way, as Speedy finally set down my breakfast. She surprised me by speaking in a soft voice with a slight mocking lilt, "Here you go, sir."

I nodded thanks, and she began her long retreat.

"Tell me about the park," I said, and Veeren nodded at my food, indicating I should eat while he talked.

I took a big bite and savored it. I don't know which I enjoyed more, the scrambled eggs, or the realization that I didn't have to wash them down with the goat turd tea.

He informed me that to the north of Chitwan National Park, the Narayani-Rapti river system formed a natural boundary. The east and north borders of the park ran parallel with the Parsa and Valmiki National Parks.

Together this large block of alluvial grasslands and subtropical deciduous forest covered over 1,370 square miles. This area was known as the Chitwan-Parsa-Valmiki Tiger Conservation Unit, or TCU for short.

Veeren's eyes lit up when he talked about the TCU.

"For centuries, this was the favorite hunting ground of the ruling class. There were no roads here—from Kathmandu, you had to come by foot."

I thought of that perilous bus ride down steep and winding roads and along terrifying ravines to get here, and I said, "That must have taken weeks."

"Yes, it did," he said, "for they didn't come alone. They traveled with a large entourage of servants, plus porters to carry everything."

He nodded, and a sad look overcame him as he added, "They came for the abundance of animals. There were so many rhinos, tigers, leopards and sloth bears that they couldn't stay away."

I reached across the table for the salt, and at the same time, a macaque darted under my arm and grabbed a handful of scrambled eggs.

"What the ...?" I stammered with a full mouth.

Veeren stood and shoed the monkey away.

"Bold little bugger, eh?" he said, almost affectionately.

After we finished our breakfast, I asked Veeren if he could guide us the next morning.

"I would be delighted," he said. "Let me show you where we can meet up in the morning."

We left the restaurant and followed a path that sloped toward the river. Farmers had terraced the fertile patches of land for rice and wheat, and we skirted along a flooded paddy until we reached an overlook.

Veeren pointed out the park entry point by a guard shack on the other side of the river. Several dugout canoes were beached on the shore on our side. "In the morning, continue on this path until you reach the boats, and a man will paddle you across the river. One of your dollars will cover the fee for you both. I will wait on the other side, by the entry post."

"You want us there real early, don't you?" asked Dee reluctantly.

He laughed. "Yes. Sunrise is at five, and you should be at the post by then. I will have your paperwork ready, and we will leave right away."

He glanced down at the river and frowned.

"And do not try to cross the river on your own — use a boat. It may not look deep, but there are mugger crocodiles in the water."

We turned to head up the hill to the main road, but a loud screeching and barking sounded close by, coming from a little further down the path, and we decided to investigate.

We came upon a small field of potato crop and saw about twenty macaques encroaching on it. They were bunched up near the edge of the field, and that's where all the screaming and grunting was coming from.

Perched before the monkeys was a larger primate that I guessed had to be a hanuman, or gray, langur (*Semnopithicus entellus*). It was a male with a gray body, black face and ears, and a long tail that looped over the back toward the head.

"That is the biggest langur I've ever seen," said Veeren.

I had read that they grew to forty pounds, but this one looked bigger than that. He was nearly three feet tall, too.

He was puffed up with adrenaline, stomping and shaking. Standing angrily before the smaller macaques — even the larger males were a third of his size — made him look even larger.

Still, some of the bigger macaque males pushed forward, teeth bared as they screeched. A bold, young male tried to go around the langur and received a bite on the shoulder.

The barks and screeches were deafening, but somehow the langur held his ground, for some reason not retreating, even when it was clear that the macaques had superior numbers.

Veeren watched with disapproval.

Finally, the macaques withdrew a few paces.

Veeren said, "If there had been a few more macaques, they would have overrun him — how terrible that would have been to witness."

The macaques noticed us standing there and decided to leave — a few dragged potato plants with them.

With all the macaques gone, I could now see that the langur wore a collar, and there was a cable attaching the collar to a stake in the ground.

"He belongs to someone," said Veeren. "That is why he did not retreat — he was not able to."

He scratched his head, rubbed his neck, and added, "They are both children of Hanuman — the monkey god. Regardless of the trouble the macaques might cause, I don't think we should set the monkeys against each other."

By the primate's feet was a bucket filled with leaves and vegetables.

"No wonder he is such a fatty," said Veeren. "In the wild they never grow this big — it is not natural."

We followed the path back to the main road and said goodbye to Veeren. I could tell that witnessing the captive langur had bothered him, and he held his head low as he walked, seemingly deep in thought.

A few moments later, we saw Speedy skipping down the road — apparently, her slow speeds were reserved for work.

She noticed us and slowed. "I saw you with Veeren," she said, stopping. "You're not going on safari with him, are you?"

"Sure," said Dee. "Why not? He's got a guide's license."

She paused and glanced around before saying, "Because he is a coward — he is terrified of tigers."

"He seems knowledgeable to me," I said.

"Well, you don't know him," she added. "He is my cousin. We all make fun of him because of his name: Veeren. It means "brave" but he is not brave at all."

I didn't want to get caught up in a family quarrel.

"We will take our chances," I said.

She smiled wickedly. "Then, I hope it is not the last chance you take—if you come across a tiger tomorrow, the last thing you will see is Veeren running away."

With that, she smirked and continued skipping down the path.

With Dee at Erawan Waterfalls National Park, Thailand. 1994.

Hanuman (or Gray) Langur (*Semnopithecus entellus*).
Habitat: Deserts, forests and rainforests. Range: Indian subcontinent.

Chapter Nine

Nāgá
(1994)

We waited in silence by the quiet river. In the early morning gloom, I imagined I could make out the crocodiles. Muggers, what a perfect name. But truthfully, it was too dark to see anything when we first arrived.

The Rapti River ran east to west, and the sunrise came at us from upstream, beyond some low hills in the distance.

The morning was hot, but it was cooler by the water.

The sky brightened, and eventually I made out four Nepalese men standing on the shore by their boats — sturdy dugout canoes.

A few other tourists arrived over the next half hour, but the men made no move to depart.

Several egrets walked along the shore.

In the trees around us parakeets and sunbirds chattered.

The sun seemed about ready to burst above the horizon when they finally loaded us into two of the boats, and the instant that golden spark of light crested the distance, we pushed off — apparently, nobody was allowed in the park before sunrise.

Pithecophilia

I scanned the water and saw no crocs, but downstream I glimpsed a family of otters at play. The rising sun reflected golden off their slick coats.

On the far shore of the river Veeren waited for us by the guard shack, and as he had said, he had our papers in hand. He had requested we each bring four liters of water, and once he confirmed we had daypacks filled with sloshing plastic jugs, we set off, walking south into the high grass.

The first thing I noticed was the humidity; in the village it had been hot, but at times a nice breeze flowed—here, we were immersed in a thick dampness.

We kept a good pace for about a mile when we came upon an observation platform. It sat only four feet above the ground, but it was high enough to offer a view over the grasslands. Tall deciduous sal trees dotted the landscape, offering only sporadic shelter from the sun.

Away from the river the temperature soared. It couldn't have been later than six o'clock, but it must have been in the nineties. My shirt was already completely soaked with sweat.

The dull drone of insects rang in my ears.

Veeren motioned for us to take a seat on one of the benches and hydrate. I drank a half-liter in one long gulp and still felt parched.

"The Terai is a floodplain habitat," he said with a sweeping motion. "The grasslands begin at the river and then sweep back for a mile or two until the dense forest begins."

The savanna seemed endless. The escalating heat had turned the morning mist into a rising haze, and I could barely make out the trees that lined the river.

Veeren continued, "The grasslands make up about twenty percent of the park. There are over fifty different types of grass— giant cane, Kans grass, Khagra reeds—and elephant grass, which can grow to twenty-five feet tall."

He glanced at the sun, which now lay fully exposed in the eastern sky. "But there is no shelter here," he said. "Come, we will walk for another mile and get into the forest."

We shouldered our daypacks and continued.

Veeren had informed us the day before that we would try to avoid other people on our walk, and I was glad for that when I spotted a line of safari vehicles in the distance, all crowded around something.

But we weren't blazing a new path; we followed a well-used game trail. I wondered how many eons had passed since its creation and how many creatures had used it.

Yet man was here, too. *Homo sapiens* have been on the Indian subcontinent for at least 65,000 years. And those early inhabitants of this area faced a challenge identical to what the early African hominins dealt with.

The first peoples to live here were food for large cats — tigers and leopards. In Africa, early man fell victim to leopard attacks, and a similar-sized feline named *Dinofelis*.

I imagined walking through this grass as an early hominin, but the thought of encountering a tiger unarmed made the hair on the back of my neck stand on end. For a moment, I wished Veeren carried a gun instead of binoculars.

It's a wonder we don't all have Ailurophobia: the persistent and excessive fear of cats.

Many people develop this disease after being attacked or witnessing someone else being attacked by a house cat, but could there be a genetic component? Is it possible that our ancestors were so terrified of the big cats that even today in our genes, or our subconscious, that dread persists?

As if Veeren could read my thoughts — or knew my fears — he crouched and pointed out a track. "Leopard," he said while scanning the trees around us. "We might get lucky and see him."

As we continued toward the tropical forest, he whispered a few facts to us. I learned that leopards co-exist with tigers but are socially subordinate and usually driven to the peripheries of a tiger's home range. And that's where we were, on the edge of the jungle.

In the back of my mind I thought of Speedy claiming Veeren to be a coward, but it didn't seem like he was afraid of the leopard at all.

In fact, as we trudged closer to the forest, he kept glancing excitedly at the trees, as if he hoped to encounter the big cat up there with a fresh kill dangling over a thick branch.

We escaped the sun when we entered the jungle, but the humidity remained with us. Veeren followed a trail and walked ahead with Dee, talking about the many uses of the Sal tree.

"This tree has been used in Ayurvedic medicine for thousands of years to treat a variety of diseases..."

His voice faded away as I drifted along, staring up at the treetops and the dangling creeper vines. I could hear the howls of some primate, and it seemed we were getting closer to it.

Loud whooping calls drew me deeper into the jungle.

In a few moments we reached a clearing with a small pool of water at the far end. Here the understory shrubs and bushes gave way, but high above, a thin canopy shielded us from the sun.

This area was frequently used by animals. Their activities had flattened the grass that surrounded the pond.

There had to be at least twenty chital deer. They stood about three feet tall with a tawny-colored upper coat covered with white spots. The throat, inner legs, ears, and tail were also white.

I watched them munching away on grasses and shrubs and noticed there were primates interspersed with the herd. A dozen langurs foraged on the ground, as well as a small troop of macaques.

I felt like we had been dropped into Kipling's *Jungle Book*.

It seemed so peaceful and calm until suddenly, a langur at the top of a tree made a series of harsh vocalizations. Everybody froze. The deer stood as one, motionless, listening with rapt attention. The langurs on the ground and the macaques also kept perfectly still.

About twenty seconds later, they continued to feed.

"That behavior is called mutualism," said Veeren. "The langur has great eyesight. He will perch on the top of a tree, and if he sees trouble approaching, he notifies the other animals. At the same time, the chital on the ground help with their highly developed sense of smell. If they get a whiff of a tiger, they will sound a warning."

"And they recognize each other's warnings?" asked Dee.

Veeren grinned. "Like their life depends on it. They work together very well, and because of that, the tiger's success rate is only between five and ten percent."

We sat quietly, watching them for another ten minutes. The langurs that foraged in the trees dropped berries as they picked off leaves to eat.

And directly under them, several deer quickly ate the berries as they hit the ground.

On the walk out, we kept our heads down and tried to knock out the two miles back to the river quickly, but this was our first big hike after a slow recovery of God knows what, and in the end, we trudged. It was a relief to collapse into the canoe to cross the Rapti River, but the walk up the hill on the other side seemed endless.

I kept silent and let my mind drift to the langurs who lived symbiotically with the chital. They seemed happy — if I can use that word — and I could have watched them frolicking all day.

It was so different from the experience of observing the captive langur in the village.

Back at the **New Nepali Friendly Café**, Speedy was nowhere in sight, and I was surprised to see the old man shuffling our way after a moment with a round of coffees.

I would rather have had a cold drink, but it was barely ten o'clock, and this was when we usually showed up for breakfast. The old man took a quick look at Veeren, smiled, and spoke to him in Hindi.

"My grandfather says the coffees are his treat for going on safari with me," translated Veeren.

"Your grandfather?" asked Dee.

Veeren blushed. "Yes, my aunt and uncle own this restaurant. They are in Kathmandu with my father right now, on business."

We ordered breakfast, relieved to see the old man had help in the kitchen, and before long, we were back in the coolness of our room, taking shelter under the mosquito net.

Over the coming days, we planned on going on morning walks with Veeren a few more times, but for now it was time to hide from the heat.

The next excursion didn't go as smoothly. We were at the river crossing on time, but there was some difficulty at the guard station that delayed us for over two hours. By the time the three of us entered the savanna, the sun was blazing in the sky.

We did not stop at the observation platform, instead pushing straight for the jungle. But by the time we got to the water hole, the animals had moved on.

I could see why: the cool morning freshness had vanished, and it seemed the flies now ruled the place.

We continued down the path, trudging through the thick jungle heat for an hour, and then spent another hour following the edge of the forest and the savanna. But it seemed all the animals had just disappeared.

Veeren said, "The chital will be laying low somewhere cool— maybe we should do the same."

Twenty minutes later, we sat in the shade of a sal tree. Veeren had led us about a half-mile into the grasslands, and then selected this tree as it grew on a slight rise.

It was closing in on midday, and a puddle of shade cast by the tree hovered as a ten-foot circle around the trunk.

Dee pointed out some large mammals moving through the grass, and I caught a glimpse of what looked like water buffalos.

"Those are gaurs," said Veeren, "they have come down from the hills to graze. They are the world's largest wild cattle."

Dee looked eager to see more animals and stood to scan the high grass around us. Veeren handed her his binoculars and she asked, "Do you think we might see a tiger?"

He chuckled. "They say a tiger is a hundred times more likely to spot you than vice versa."

"But still, we might, right?"

Veeren shook his head. "At this time of the day, it would be exceptionally rare. And it would not be good."

"Why's that?" she asked, crestfallen.

"Well, during the day, the tigers normally stay in areas of the park that are off-limits to tourists. They sleep until evening — and then they come out to hunt."

He paused and looked at us. "For a tiger to be out hunting in the middle of the day can only mean he is desperate."

Dee nodded. "But they might come through this area at night?"

"Oh yes," said Veeren, "at night, you would not want to be here."

He lowered his voice and said, "At night, sometimes you are not safe anywhere. Tigers in Chitwan National Park have attacked foreigners on night drives, and across the river, in my village — people have been attacked there, too, walking home at night."

I said, "It must be tough living alongside such a dangerous animal."

"It is a challenge," he said, "but it is not impossible if you stay indoors at night. Most tiger kills are within the park's boundaries, less than a half-mile from the forest edge, away from humans. But today, there are more than eighty breeding tigers in the park, and as their numbers grow, their territories begin to overlap with that of humans."

Then, Veeren surprised me as his face lit up, and he said, "But my problem is, I love tigers! I can't stay away. They are majestic, and they fascinate me — and I am lucky to live in one of the most incredible tiger habitats in the world."

I took a sip of water and asked, "But are you afraid of them?"

Veeren stared over the high grass. He nodded at a lone gaur bull who was quickly moving through the grass in the direction of the others — toward the river.

In a moment, he was gone, and Veeren said, "I'm not afraid of healthy tigers."

Dee sat next to me. She said, "You fear the desperate ones?"

He nodded, and we waited for him to collect his thoughts. Veeren took a long swig of water and then began his tale.

"Ten years ago, my father had to leave our home for three months to work at a village about 150 miles from here. This village was next to the Royal Bardia National Park.

"After work each day, my father had to walk a remote trail through the jungle to get to the place where he slept. And he dreaded this walk because there was a man-eating tiger in the area, and nobody knew when or where it would strike next."

Veeren looked me in the eye and said, "This tiger's name was Bhangay, and he had already killed two people."

Dee leaned forward eagerly. "What happened?"

Veeren took a breath. "One night, as my father walked alone, he heard a loud crashing behind him. He jumped in fear and fled. He dared only one quick glance behind him, but in it he saw something huge and orange and fearful.

"The next day, a young girl was killed on the very trail. The village organized a hunt, and in a few days, the tiger was captured."

Dee looked at me; Veeren was sweating. It was obvious this story was getting more difficult for him, but he continued.

"This tiger was so old that he had outlived his place in the jungle. His canine teeth were missing or broken, and he had a broken right leg. Most of his claws had been ripped out, too, perhaps in a fight with a rival.

"This poor animal had to drag itself after its prey, and then cause terrible suffering while it struggled to kill it. There was none of the grace and quickness of a typical tiger kill. I feel so bad for the young girl, its last victim. The thought of that desperate creature crawling after her still fills me with terror.

"From the day my father told me that story, when I was eleven, until now, there has been a fear in me of encountering one of those dreadful tigers."

We let his story settle. Then Dee asked, "And where is Bhangay now?"

Veeren gave a weak smile. "He lives in the Kathmandu Zoo. After killing three people, he could not be released, but they have helped him heal and gave him a nice enclosure."

We saw a few rhinos in the distance. They were a good mile off in the opposite direction of the guard booth.

"Next time, I will make sure we see rhinos up close," said Veeren.

On our third outing, we had no delay at the guard post. The heat had let up too, and we enjoyed our morning walk. Veeren led us across the savanna to another jungle clearing — this one lay at the base of a small hill with a flat rock at the top.

From our perch on the rock, we could see a herd of about a dozen chital with a few hog deer mixed in. Like before, a troop of langurs foraged alongside the deer, with a few sentinels in the trees.

Doves cooed from the bushes nearby, and a pair of black drongos kept swooping above us, making me wonder if we were near their nest.

On the far side of the clearing lay a carcass.

Veeren peered through his binoculars and said, "It's a wild boar."

Suddenly one of the langur sentinels let out a rumbling scream, and one of the hog deer jumped and fled the clearing. The chital on the ground stopped all movement.

A moment later, two langurs descended from the trees, one chasing the other. The first one dropped almost twenty-five feet before grabbing a branch, and once on the ground it fled the clearing with a few bipedal hops.

With a loud grunt, the other returned to the top of the tree.

We left the clearing, and on the trail again, Veeren pointed out different tracks that we came upon. We saw lots of pangolin and porcupine prints and several striped hyena tracks.

Veeren directed us toward the savanna again, and we left the jungle in the hope of finally seeing a rhino up close. On the way, we

sighted five chitals, running single file and following a path that
skirted the grasslands.

"You see how they travel with a distance of two or three times
their length between them?" asked Veeren. "That's an antipredator
measure because it doesn't allow a tiger to attack more than one at
a time."

The amount of effort each animal put into avoiding tigers and
leopards was sobering, but weirdly, I envied them. I've always
wished that instead of having to fear violent members of our society
- murderers, thieves or child molesters - I would rather have a large
predator to contend with.

Something fierce and tangible that I could battle.

Maybe the beast would sense when you are tired of life or weak,
like a wolf watching a flock of sheep. Or perhaps it would just be a
random predator that you always had to be ready to fight.

I remembered the lions of Capron Park coughing on a hot
summer night when I was a kid. At times, I thought they sounded
closer than they should and wondered if one of them had escaped.

Maybe that was the first time I truly sensed a predator out there,
an African lion prowling through the neighborhoods of Attleboro,
Massachusetts.

I am not sure why the notion appeals to me.

Perhaps it's because in modern society, predators are hidden.
They live among us. There's no way to tell how dangerous a man
is by just looking at him.

If given a choice, I'd rather face an obvious danger – one that I
see coming.

Of course, as soon as I glimpsed a tiger coming at me, I might
recant.

But when I am home, safe, I yearn for that predator again.

Veeren explained another anti-predator practice used by the
chital while we walked. When the langur had spooked the hog
deer, and it fled, the chital had remained in place—they flee in
groups to cause more confusion.

I wondered if we would flee as a group if trouble came our way.

We cut across the grasslands, stopping twice to take shelter under a lone tree. Each time we scanned the grass with Veeren's binoculars. Even though there are over six hundred one-horned rhinos in Chitwan, they can be tough to spot in the high grass.

About a mile away, Veeren sighted a few with his binoculars, and while we walked in their direction, he told us a few facts about them.

"The Indian rhinoceros," he explained, "at one time ranged across the entire expanse of the Indo-Gangetic Plain, an area that encompassed most of eastern and northern India. Farming and excessive hunting reduced their range to eleven sites in northern India and southern Nepal."

He sighed, "Additionally, poachers kill them for their horns — less than 3,000 survive worldwide."

Then he motioned for us to be silent as we closed in on them.

There were a half-dozen sal trees near us, twenty or thirty feet apart, and one sizeable rhino-apple tree.

Veeren was whispering a few facts about the rhino apple when suddenly we heard rustling as something large moved our way through the high grass.

"That way," said Veeren, as he indicated the closest tree.

We quickly hurried there, and then Veeren and I helped Dee scramble up the tree. The rustling was getting closer as Veeren gave me ten fingers to assist my climb.

And as I reached down to help him up into the tree, the rhino's thick grey-brown body came into view just behind him.

The tree was less than a foot wide and didn't have many lower branches, but we managed to huddle safely about ten feet above the prehistoric-looking creature.

I knew a few facts about the Indian rhino, too. They can grow to over eight thousand pounds, with the average male weighing just under five. Their horn is made of keratin, like a human fingernail, and grows to about ten inches tall.

This one was a male — with a good-sized horn. He drifted in circles around us, and he seemed to like the shade under our tree.

A few minutes later, three more rhinos emerged from the grass. They all made a pass at the nearby rhino apple, sniffing the ground for last year's fruit, before moving on

The beast lingering below us seemed in no rush to leave. I stared down at that horn and wondered if I would end up impaled on it if I fell from the tree; or if the rhino would trample me to death.

Dee's foot slipped off a branch and she let out a curse.

The rhino grunted in surprise and shot a stream of urine backward at least ten feet.

A few seconds later, he settled down again. With his poor eyesight, he hadn't spotted us above him.

"We might as well get comfortable," said Veeren as he climbed above Dee and wedged himself in a fork.

Dee and I did the same, and soon we were digging into our packs for our water bottles. Veeren pulled out some brown bread and a hunk of yak cheese and shared it with us.

Below us, a myna bird had landed on the rhino's back and was hopping around, picking off ticks — more mutualism.

Again, I imagined myself as an early hominin — a *Sahelanthropus* perhaps — fleeing a large beast and getting stuck in a tree on the African plain. I don't know if I've ever been happier. All my troubles condensed into the dangerous beast below me.

My legs eventually began cramping, and I was relieved an hour later, when we were back in the jungle, walking on the trail. Our excursion had taken us several miles, and Veeren thought it best to stay under the shelter of the trees until we got closer to the guard post.

We walked along quietly, listening to the birds. Of course, I also had my ears attuned to the call of a primate.

Eventually, we came to the clearing we had visited on our first walk — the one with the small watering hole.

Five male chital browsed under a tree in which a half-dozen langurs were feeding in the treetops. The bucks donned three-pronged antlers that were nearly three feet long.

We stayed with them for about ten minutes, but just as we prepared to leave, one of the langur sentinels began sounding off loud grunts and barks.

Then he let out a rumbling alarm call that set my hair on end.

Veeren scanned the edge of the clearing, about a hundred feet away, but could see nothing. Shrubs and grass sparsely covered the near distance, but we could see nothing there, either.

Yet the langur would not stop sounding off, and the frozen stance of the chital underscored that they were taking his warning seriously.

The heavy sense of dread that had accompanied me back when I was lost in Sumatra came over me again. I kept thinking I saw something in the high grass.

A flicker of orange.

I could tell Veeren took the langur's warning seriously as well. He was sweating profusely as his eyes swept over the grass. Several times he glanced up into the tree, where he could see the langur looking in the direction of the grasslands.

Suddenly the chital were fleeing, as one, with high leaps and their white tails flagging until they disappeared.

We were now the only ones on the ground.

Veeren appeared undecided on what to do. He could see nothing, but the damn langur in the tree still wouldn't shut up.

"Could it be a tiger?" asked Dee.

"Let's hope not," whispered Veeren.

After a long minute, Veeren said, "I can't figure why that langur keeps screaming, but we can't stay here all day. We must continue into the savanna — that is the way to the guard post."

Unfortunately, that was also where the langur's stare was directed.

As we set out, Veeren looked jumpy.

I wondered whether he would desert us if we saw a tiger.

The langur would not stop calling out his warning, and it was unnerving. In my head, it rang like a fire alarm.

Veeren pointed to the grasslands and said, "Go that way," in a barely audible voice.

Dee went first, then me, and then Veeren, whose eyes continuously scanned the edge of the clearing.

After a few steps, he paused and glanced back at the langur in the treetop, and then ahead of us again, perplexed.

He caught a flicker of movement in front of us.

Recognition dawned in his eyes, and he yelled at Dee, who was still walking. "Stop!"

The next few seconds seemed to pass in slow motion.

Dee turned and, at that moment, twisted her ankle. She came down on her knee and fell over onto her hip.

Directly in front of her, a cobra rose, fanning its hood.

Veeren yelled, "Nāgá!" and dashed forward, around Dee, to the snake.

It was a king cobra, about thirteen feet long.

It was olive green with black and white bands. Its black tongue darted out as it loomed over Dee.

I tried to seize Dee's shoulders and pull her back.

At the same time, Veeren grabbed the snake's thick tail and heaved its entire body back and over his head.

The effort brought him to the ground, and as he lay there, he watched the cobra sail over him, slowly twisting around.

The snake hit the ground and spun around as Veeren was scrambling away.

Then he stood next to us, breathing heavily, and we watched as the cobra took one last look at us before slithering into the high grass.

Dee smiled, still trying to catch her breath, and said, "That's the bravest thing I've ever seen anyone do."

Veeren blushed. "Madam, I may be afraid of tigers, but I am not a coward."

Back at the restaurant, we ordered a big breakfast. Nothing stirs up an appetite like an adventure with a taste of danger! Today's walk was our last; in the evening, we would board another sketchy overnight bus — this one to Kathmandu — and then we planned to fly to Singapore.

The restaurant was busy. Two men and a woman were unloading a truck full of supplies, making trips to the kitchen and back. The men looked like brothers, and I figured they were Veeren's uncle and father.

Speedy was there, too. She stuck out her tongue when she passed Veeren, but he was on a high and only grinned back.

The grandfather shuffled over to us, got us seated, then returned a few minutes later with coffees.

By that time, the truck bed was empty, and the three adults were chatting by the kitchen entrance. The woman nudged Speedy, indicating she should give grandpa a break and take our order.

I prodded Veeren. "Tell your grandfather about what happened today." He blushed slightly and then began speaking in Hindi.

Behind him, I could see Speedy coming at us at half speed.

Veeren spoke in his soft voice, the one he used in the bush. I couldn't grasp what he was saying until he said the word, "Nāgá," and suddenly, the old man stepped back and shouted, "Nāgá!"

The three adults quickly walked over to our table, thinking there was something wrong. One of the men glanced under the table.

"Is there a snake?" he asked.

Now Veeren was really blushing. He held up his hands, indicating everything was all right, and said, "No. There is no snake."

Seeing that his relatives understood English, I introduced myself.

"Veeren has been taking us on walking safaris," I added, "and this morning, after being treed by a rhino, we had an encounter with a cobra."

"It was a king cobra, I believe," said Dee.

Veeren nodded and continued telling the events of our day.

He started in English, but when he realized his grandfather couldn't follow, he switched to Hindi. He also included animal sounds and movements to his tale, and he recounted events so lively that I found I didn't need to understand his words. When he glanced up and made a rough grunt, I knew he was talking about the langur, and the fleeing chital were apparent as well.

He said the word "Nāgá," and again, everyone went wide-eyed.

When he made the motion of grabbing the snake's tail and heaving the body backward, I noticed one of the men sucked in his breath — and I knew that was Veeren's father.

And then everyone was talking at once, excited.

Veeren's father said to me, "You, please. Tell me this story in English." And I gave them my version. I didn't think the old man could understand many of my words, but he smiled and nodded the whole way through, regardless.

Speedy began listening with a cynical expression but softened near the end. But I could tell she didn't want to let her cousin entirely off the hook.

She stared at him and said, "But he doesn't even know how to handle a snake — it's amazing he didn't get bit."

Dee smiled at Veeren and said, "That's what made his act so brave."

She glanced at Veeren's father and said, "You really did give him the perfect name."

Eventually we ordered, and everyone went about their day. Veeren's eyes glowed with pride, and his parents seemed very pleased with him.

We thanked him for his guiding service, and he walked off to escape the heat of the day.

Dee sipped her coffee, and I stirred mine while staring across the river at the grasslands. I decided to jot down a few notes about our safari but dropped the pen accidentally.

When I glanced under the table to find it, I noticed a young macaque huddled in a bush about five feet away.

A few other tables were occupied, and he was furtively watching to see if anyone dropped a scrap. He caught my eye, and we stared at each other for a full minute.

I gave him a conspiratorial wink.

Then he disappeared back into the bush, out of sight.

Indian rhinoceros at Chitwan
National Park. 1994.

Chacma Baboon (*Papio ursinus*).
Habitat: Savanna woodlands and forests. Range: Southern Africa.

Chapter Ten

Shirley
(1996)

*O*ne of the benefits of lacking a highly developed default brain network that distracts you all the time is that you can focus more of your brain on the task at hand. A few years ago, I took a driver safety class, and the instructor asked how many of us dedicated one hundred percent of our attention to driving.

About half the class raised their hands and he chuckled.

"First of all," he said, "if there are other passengers in the car, then forget about it. You can't focus completely with others talking to you. So maybe you never drive with passengers. Okay, but is the radio on? News, sports, even music can pull your attention away from driving."

Now I was realizing that one of the biggest distractions we have — one that the instructor didn't even mention — is our own default mind.

How many times had I been driving along when I suddenly found myself getting mad or anxious because of some wandering thought in my head? And that, in turn, affected my driving: Maybe I slowly accelerated or suddenly became more liable to slip into road rage.

How nice it seemed to be an animal that didn't get its thoughts tangled up in internal debates. Would there be self-doubt? Possibly, but not on the same level.

Once while camping in Zimbabwe's Hwange National Park, I had an opportunity to observe an animal while it focused all its attention on a possible victim.

Unfortunately, I was the potential prey.

After a day of driving the park's dusty roads in search of elephants, I was in my tent, trying to fall asleep. My body felt like it was still moving, as if the swaying vehicle was still connected to me, and at two a.m. I found myself wide awake, listening to insects.

It was a hot night, so I sat up and unzipped my tent.

I lit a candle and decided to update my journal on the last few days. I had scribbled down a few pages when I paused and looked up.

The crickets had gone silent.

I glanced through the opening of my tent, into the black night, and twenty feet away, I spied a shadow.

I squinted at it, and as if on cue, the silhouette crept my way.

At ten feet, I could see it was a lioness. An adult, with a beautiful tawny coat. She was of a good size. I would guess three hundred pounds, and I could see her tail dancing behind her as she stared at me.

If I'd had my wits, I might have sat up and quickly zipped up the tent, not sure what good that would have done, but I was too engrossed watching her move—hypnotically—in my direction.

She silently glided the next few paces.

My heart raced, and it fired off at double speed when she passed the threshold of my tent and set her front two feet inside.

I couldn't move.

My vision began to constrict into a tightening circle.

Behind me I heard footsteps. They were whooshing in my ears. I feared another lion had showed up and only later realized the sound was the rushing of my own blood.

She paused and glanced at my flickering candle. After blinking once, she turned to me. I stared into her eyes for what seemed an eternity, hoping to see compassion, or maybe curiosity, but I could read nothing.

Her glance was alien to me.

Oscar might have watched me with a similar stare, but the lion's mind was so different from mine that I couldn't fathom her motivation; other than knowing a sudden action from me could provoke a response from her.

With Oscar, I would have known in an instant. I think I get simian motives: What he might fear or make him protective, what he might consider food. We're family — both primates — after all.

But stuck alone in my tent that night, I didn't know what to expect from a bold lioness. Clearly, I was no Tarzan. And maybe I should have paid more attention when Jim Fowler climbed out of the jeep on *Wild Kingdom*. But soon, that wouldn't matter.

While my vision continued to telescope into ever smaller circles, I felt I was about to pass out and then get eaten.

I dropped to one elbow, and as I desperately tried to fight blacking out, the lioness took one step closer to me and sniffed my neck.

I sighed in resignation and sank to the ground.

I could vaguely see her, my beautiful lioness, as she gave me a last long look, then turned and walked away.

Her amber gaze, and that of the apes I'd encountered over the years, kept me on the move, wanting more. Because out of all the things I had encountered in the world — fabulous ruins, majestic mountain ranges, pristine jungles — nothing shook me more than the stare of a wild animal.

After our trip to Asia, Dee and I returned to New Hampshire, and both worked almost non-stop. Dee waitressed at a Nashua restaurant called *Michael Timothy's*. I painted houses with a small crew by day, and at night typed up my travel articles.

By the next winter we were off to Africa.

Even when we were in Asia, I couldn't wait to travel Africa with her.

Don't get me wrong; I loved traveling in Asia. But most of my experiences in Asia seemed to take place in my head: meditation, Buddhism, even my day to day interactions with people. I drifted along serenely, feeling connected to those around me.

And I've had my fair share of adventures there, too. Like when I got lost in Sumatra and was surrounded by orangutans, or more recently, the walking safaris in Chitwan National Park.

But in Africa, I seemed to live in my stomach in an adrenaline-based world that made me want to take chances. In Asia, I might trek through the mountains, but in Africa, I would climb them. And in Asia, I might go on a guided safari, but in Africa, I would go off on solo full moon hikes — many of which resulted in me getting chased by an animal.

I really couldn't wait to introduce Dee to that rumble in the gut. Or the feeling that accompanies listening to tribal drums that makes you want to dance with abandon.

I yearned for the wave of excitement and fear that washes over you when you are standing alone in the night, and you suddenly realize there is a large animal in the shrubs right next to you.

In Asia, I would have retreated to my bungalow and wondered what creature was lurking in the dark, but in Africa, I would creep through the thickets until I got a glimpse of it.

Mind versus soul? I don't know other than to say when I was in Africa, I always felt there was a deep, restless part of me that had woken the moment my plane touched down. And like a bear coming out of a long hibernation, that voice shouted that it had been asleep too long to remain idle for one minute more. It was hungry.

Dee and I began our first trip to the continent in Malawi. We made our way to Lake Malawi and then island-hopped in sea kayaks so I could write an article about Kayak Africa's operation in Lake Malawi National Park.

Over the next month we traveled south, through Mozambique, to Zimbabwe. There we met my brother, David, and my mom, Patricia, who had flown out to spend a month with us.

Suddenly I was traveling with family and a mate. Have to say, I felt a bit like an alpha. I might even have had a swagger to my walk.

And that might be why I slipped into aggressive behavior, which isn't cool because alphas are supposed to control the space. They're supposed to stay calm under pressure.

We were camped at the Victoria Falls Campground, getting ready to raft the Zambezi River the next morning. I knew the camping area well, having stayed there on previous trips to southern Africa.

You can hear the falls from twenty-five miles away. Our campground was less than a mile from them, and the rumble was so constant I felt like it lived in my chest.

Africa's fourth-largest river, the Zambezi, thunders into a deep chasm where it is over a half-mile wide, and a great surge of water vapor soars heavenward as if trying to escape the earth.

You can see the cloud as it rises thirteen hundred feet above the water-pounded rocks. Some of it trickled down on us as a light rain whenever the wind shifted.

Earlier in the day we had walked along the grassy precipice where the land fell away before the falls. We stared at it head-on, feeling the deep growl of the earth before us. I was so pleased to have my mom and brother with me, standing drenched by my side.

And there was my girlfriend — my fiancé by then — whom I photographed kissing one of the numerous rainbows that floated over the mist.

Livingstone had been here in 1855. The famed Scot was the first European to see the falls, which is fitting considering his obsession with the Zambezi River.

He said his Sotho guides called the waterfall *Mosi-oa-Tunya*, The Smoke That Thunders, and they were reluctant to approach it because they had a sacral fear of the place.

At night, when I sensed the ground shaking under my mat, I understood their trepidation.

On full moons, the rising mist is painted silver, and the plateau becomes a magical shimmering savanna.

During those days, the campground is often full of overland vehicles and their passengers, who hop the park fence — the national park is closed at night — and make their way to the grassy meadow that faces the falls. I've had a few good reunions there over the years.

But the full moon was a few weeks away, and we couldn't linger that long, so the silver meadow would have to wait for the next visit.

We had been at the campground for a few days and were constantly on guard from animals that would steal our food. At night we stored everything in a cooler that was shut up tight in our rented Land Rover, but whenever we made meals or lounged around our fire after eating, we became targets.

It started the first morning when I sat unaware, enjoying the early morning coolness. Birds sang around me, fluttering on the dew-laden branches. Higher up in the treetops, I could hear some form of primate rustling about, although I had yet to catch a glimpse of it.

I had cooked some breakfast sausage and had a coffeepot bubbling on rekindled coals. I was about to remove the coffeepot to make a cup when I noticed movement from the corner of my eye.

I turned to see a grey monkey — a vervet (*Chlorocebus pygerythrus*) — running at me. His black face was fringed with white, and he stood about twenty inches tall. He looked like a miniature human the way he sprinted with his arms pumping by his sides.

I smiled at the bizarre sight until I realized that his eyes were fixated — one hundred percent — on something behind me.

I turned just in time to see his right hand shoot out to grab my five-pound bag of sugar and shouted, "Hey!"

He clutched it tightly and climbed — with one hand and two feet — up an acacia tree.

I stood at the base of the tree, watching him gorge himself, and as unhappy as I was at the prospect of drinking black coffee for the rest of the week, there was another part of my mind that marveled at the incredibly vivid blue of the monkey's testicles.

A flutter of wings alerted me to several lilac-breasted rollers that had swooped down to the table and were rapidly pecking up all our breakfast sausages.

I gave up on the sugar and moved toward the table, but stopped when a shadow passed overhead, and then a black eagle dropped down out of the sky, right above me. I wasn't sure if he was going for the sausage or the rollers — or me, for that matter.

And thus began our battle against the animals.

It seemed all the critters in the vicinity were determined to get our food: Eagles, hawks, kites, monkeys, warthogs, even hyenas. They all came around looking for scraps, stealing what they could, around mealtime.

Some came by so often that we named them, like a young warthog we called Walter, and a hyena we dubbed Randy.

But by far, the biggest threats came from the baboons.

Chacma baboons (*Papio ursinus*) frequented the campground, and we had been given a warning from one ranger that they could be "cheeky."

One baboon that visited us several times a day was a big male. He weighed close to one hundred pounds and had fangs that measured an inch and a half. I thought this was a female at first; I was used to seeing male baboons with manes, and the chacma males are maneless. But then he got closer, and I realized my mistake.

The first morning he approached us, I admired the deep brown coat that covered his muscular body. He had a scraggy patch of hair along the nape of his neck that made him look like a ruffian.

David was sitting in a camp chair next to me and watched the big baboon drift from campsite to campsite. He seemed mellow and secretive. But then another baboon approached him and tried to take away a roll he'd just scored from some Swiss campers.

Suddenly he became ferocious, slapping the ground and half-lunging forward, displaying his canines. We watched him more closely after that.

He moved like a magnet to any food, slowing down when he got close and evaluating the various campsites from behind a bush. He seemed to melt into the foliage until he was ready to make a move.

A few times the campers caught sight of him, and he'd retreat just a little and occupy himself otherwise until the humans forgot about him. I marveled at how convincing he was when he wanted someone to think he had given up.

Then he'd go for whatever edible bits had been exposed. It didn't matter what it was: chips, vegetables, even a steak was fair game.

"He sure is sneaky," I said. "If you didn't watch him closely, you'd never know what he was up to."

David chuckled and told me about a girl he had begun dating, who would get drunk and then blame anything she did in that state on Shirley—a name she used to refer to her drunk self. In other words, she would accept no blame at all for her drunken actions.

"'Shirley did it, not me,' she'd say, and then pretend it never happened."

"That's a huge red flag," I told him.

He laughed at that and sighed, "Yeah, I know."

He watched the baboon creep closer to an unsuspecting camper who had just taken out his cooler. He added, "She's a bit sneaky, too."

From then on, we referred to the baboon as Shirley.

Over the coming days, Shirley got bolder and bolder, and on one occasion, he chased Dee and my mother as they returned from washing the vegetables and salad greens at the water tap. When Shirley confronted them, they fearfully dropped half the produce they'd been carrying.

Now he knew they were easy targets and waited for them as mealtime approached. As soon as I opened the cooler, he would come around, suddenly appearing from under a bush, his small brown eyes watching behind the downward-sloping face.

The night before we were to raft the Zambezi, the ladies went to the tap with some dishes and the vegetables that were to go with our dinner.

I had my brother accompany them.

Unfortunately, Shirley put on a scary show. He marched straight at them, fangs exposed. I'd hoped just having another human along would deter Shirley, but it didn't.

They beat a hasty retreat to our site and only lost Shirley when he stopped to grab a dropped cucumber.

The next morning, I asked David to carry a pocket full of rocks, and if Shirley came around, he was to scare the baboon off by throwing them at him. I decided we should go on the offensive.

In New Hampshire, David had played baseball for Hollis High School and later for an infamous softball team known as The Pounders. He had a strong arm and was accurate.

As expected, when Patricia and Dee returned from washing the produce, Shirley stepped forward and made a beeline straight for them. They were only thirty feet from our tents, but Shirley headed them off and stood in the dirt road in front of our site, waiting.

David stepped in front of the ladies, cocked his arm, and threw a rock that whizzed past the baboon on the left, about a foot off the ground.

A warning shot across the bow.

If he'd been a batter, it would have been a perfect strike.

Shirley stopped and glared at David, and I found myself drawn into his stare. It seemed Shirley's entire body was condensed into that glower.

After a moment, the baboon looked over his shoulder and barked a command, then continued moving in their direction. Around us, I could see other baboons now heading our way.

I knew we weren't going to win the battle. I grabbed a frying pan and threw it at Shirley. He nimbly jumped out of the way, but in the moment that he was distracted, I shouted, "Everybody in the Land Rover."

The vehicle was off to the side of the road, a few feet away, and before Shirley returned his focus on David or the women, we were all safely inside.

From that safety, we made our breakfast, which turned out to be cereal instead of bacon and eggs.

Then we left for the day.

I grew up rafting New England rivers like the Kennebec and the Penobscot. I thought those experiences might prepare me for the Zambezi, but I was wrong.

Those rivers are cold, the waters from the Kennebec being released from a dam, and we often wore wet suits. And there were always rocks you had to watch out for if you fell out of the raft.

After the Zambezi River plunges over Victoria Falls, it flows through a deep gorge, into twenty-four major rapids. Twenty-three are grade five, and then there's one grade six—considered un-runnable unless you're in a kayak—just to keep everyone humble.

It takes a full day to run them all.

The stretch of rapids is widely considered the best commercial one-day rafting trip in the world. We were there just after the rainy season, so the rapids were the biggest they'd be all year.

The gorge is deep, so even though some of the waves appear gigantic, there's no danger of hitting rocks except if you get swept near the banks. And there are no hippos or crocs in the water unless you count an occasional dead one that got swept over the falls.

But the speed of the water, the enormous waves, and the roar of the river are still terrifying.

We began by hiking down into the gorge, to a point at the base of the mighty falls. It was so loud there that we could only communicate through sign language.

Our first rapid was called Boiling Point. I stared at it from the shore, not quite accepting the fact that we were going to enter the river there.

The four of us climbed into the raft with a guide and four others. David and I were in the front, and Patricia and Dee in the back. We managed to make it through the first few rapids unscathed, but when we hit a major rapid called The Devil's Toilet Bowl, we flipped.

It all seemed to happen in slow motion as the raft slowly ascended into the air until there was a good five feet between the bottom of the boat and the water. All of us fell backward, out of the raft — bewildered looks and arms flailing.

We regrouped down the river where the water was calmer, and for the next few hours we worked our way downstream.

But when we hit a series of rapids called The Three Sisters, the craft dropped into a hole in the river and was folded in half. An oar stowed on the side broke in two, and one section connected with my mom.

We feared she might have broken her arm, but it seemed fine after examining it on a long straight-a-way between rapids. We lay back and caught our breath while we watched the thin ribbon of blue that stretched between the high rock walls of the gorge.

And the rapids kept piling up. I thought they would never end.

In the late afternoon, the raft rolled over a submerged boulder, and as it pulled away, Dee was sucked right out of the back of the raft and disappeared.

We all scanned the water for what seemed an eternity until she popped up thirty yards away.

We finished with a few beers that left me woozy when we did the big hike up and out of the ravine.

It had been quite a day for all of us. Patricia had a bad bruise where the oar had hit her, and Dee had gotten a bit water-logged during her submersion.

As we all limped into camp, the last thing we wanted to do was deal with Shirley.

He watched us approach from the shade of an acacia tree, his eyes never leaving the bags of food we had picked up at the market. Eventually, he slowly swaggered our way. Casually, like the idea had just come to him.

My brother sighed as he picked up a few rocks on the road. He hesitated, waiting until the baboon had entered our site before he threw it.

But his throw was strong, and at only twenty feet away, I thought he might hit the baboon this time.

Yet Shirley acted as if he were moving in slow motion. When the rock was about to hit him, the baboon simply dropped his shoulder, and the rock hurtled by.

Watching it felt like a scene from the movie "The Matrix," where the main character, Neo, dodges a dozen bullets by slowing down time and effortlessly twisting out of the way.

It suddenly dawned on me how dangerous the baboon might be once provoked. Those fangs looked horribly threatening. All of a sudden, I remembered a few campfire stories I had heard about violent baboons.

Shirley barked out a call to the other members of his troop, whom I could see moving in our direction.

Now he was only fifteen feet away. His eyes never left the food, and he was barely paying attention to David, who was about to let loose another rock.

But when my brother cocked his arm back to throw again, time stopped for me - like I had tapped into the baboon's ability to seemingly slow the passage of time. The moment stretched as if it was made of warm, soft rubber.

Suddenly I was not in Zimbabwe, but in Panama, where angry young men with yellow eyes were hurling rocks at the soldiers trying to maintain the barricades.

I was there again. Watching fearfully as the protestors shook the barriers, and the policemen glanced sideways at each other nervously.

I felt nauseous and thought I might get sick.

Angry shouting filled the air, which was thick with the smell of burning tires. I could hear an alarm blaring somewhere.

While my mind was flooded with these images, my brother, poised timelessly with his arm in mid-throw, connected both worlds.

In Panama I had compared humans with chimps and felt my species was the one lacking morals.

All my life I had been drawn to primates, but suddenly I realized I was actively trying to hurt one. We were the aggressors. How had that happened? Was this the price of being an alpha?

I realized I didn't want to hurt Shirley for any reason.

My brother was protecting us, but I could tell his heart wasn't in it. He had a gentle soul, and I knew he didn't want to hurt the animal.

"Hold on," I said, and David lowered his arm.

Panama slowly faded to the back of my mind, but I could still feel a dozen yellow eyes on me.

We had just entered our campsite and faced the baboon across the small dirt road that ran through the campground. Shirley bared his teeth as he approached, but when he saw David lower his arm, he stopped.

I was relieved to see Patricia quickly take the two food bags, toss them into the Land Rover, and then get inside herself.

David, Dee and I remained, facing the baboon head on.

It took Shirley only a moment to see the food was gone.

I could swear the baboon shrugged, but maybe that was me reading something that was not there — anthropomorphizing again.

But Shirley did determine that we no longer had any food and began to look elsewhere.

Shirley was only taking advantage of the opportunities placed before him. It wasn't personal. He did not like or dislike us. He only wanted the food that, as far as he could see, was readily available.

I felt faint as he walked away.

That night we grilled steaks over a grate on our fire. The buns, condiments, and chips we kept in the Land Rover until we were ready.

And while the steaks sizzled, we sat in a circle around them, on guard.

I had yet to see a baboon take anything directly off a fire, but I was taking no chances.

In fact, I was ravenous, and a primal side of me was ready to defend the meat—regardless of all the drama we'd recently gone through.

My stomach growled as I scanned the bushes for Shirley.

Three thoughts echoed in my head as I looked over our campsite—the alpha mantra: territory, food, and family.

By the time the steaks were ready, night had fallen.

I cut off a large chunk, burning my fingers as I held it and tore at it with my teeth. My hands and teeth flashed in the firelight as the meat disappeared.

Although the night was black, it was too early for the stars to shine fully.

When later I stepped into the Land Rover, the interior light came on, and in the mirror's reflection I saw a primitive sight. The warm grease had run down my face, dripping onto my chin, and stuck to my whiskers.

It had mixed with the day's dust, been smeared a few times, and now looked like war paint.

I almost didn't recognize myself.

In the darkness, I washed at the water tap. While drying my face, I watched a lone kudu buck silently saunter through the campground. He paused beside a large acacia tree, about thirty feet away, and I decided to see how close I could get to him.

Kudus are one of Africa's largest antelopes, and I guessed this one to weigh at least six hundred pounds. He had a black beard that crept down his neck and beautiful, spiraling horns that made two complete turns as they ascended.

I tiptoed, using the great acacia that he was standing by to block his view of me.

A bright sliver of a sharp-horned moon hung above us.

When I was less than ten feet away, the buck stepped nervously and began glancing around. I don't know if he heard me or smelled me, but he knew some creature was close.

Beyond him, on a picnic table, I spotted Shirley the baboon sitting there, watching us.

I took out my flashlight.

Then I leaned around the tree so I could see the kudu, and right before he got a glimpse of me, I turned the flashlight on and off quickly.

The buck nervously blinked.

I took the opportunity to step up close to the tree and behind it so that he couldn't see me.

I noticed Shirley blinking as well, but the baboon shook his head and continued to watch me. I'd piqued his curiosity.

I was wary of the kudu's legs because they are great kickers, and also of his horns, afraid he might gouge me if he glimpsed me behind the tree, so I moved with stealth.

Shirley watched my every move like there might be a feast waiting at the end. Maybe he thought I was stalking the kudu.

I wondered if he expected me to get kicked.

I pointed the flashlight at the antelope's eyes and turned it on and off again.

The kudu stood stunned, blinking into the darkness. I heard his breathing quicken. I could smell his exhalation. The gleaming slice of moonlight silhouetted him, and I watched his majestic horns cut in front of the stars.

I reached around the tree, extending my hand forward until it touched the kudu along its back. My fingers floated a few inches from the white vertical stripes that ran through the light gray hair.

Shirley leaned forward, appearing excited to see what would happen next.

Several times I gave the kudu a gentle pat, and then I just let my hand sit there. I could now *feel* the animal breathing and tense up every now and then.

But otherwise, for some reason, he seemed to accept me.

Shirley also seemed to relax; he sat back and just observed us.

I tried to lose myself in the moment: listening to the crickets, feeling the gentle breeze, and smelling the vegetation around us.

I tried to shrug off my expectations.

And while my hand lay on the antelope, my eyes eventually settled on Shirley, and we held each other's stare.

As usual, I wondered what was in the primate's mind — and I suddenly understood.

It was me. Shirley was concentrating on what I was doing with the kudu, what my intentions were, and might they lead to food?

And to that end, he was watching, listening, smelling, and thinking about me, and putting that all into an assessment.

I could see the curiosity in his eyes and wondered if he considered my actions abnormal.

The buck fidgeted for a moment, and our eyes went to it, but after he settled, I met Shirley's curious stare again.

And we stayed like that for what seemed an eternity, sharing the moment.

Beneath our feet, the earth rumbled from the pounding of Victoria Falls, and above us countless stars glittered powerfully. But I only stared into Shirley's eyes while I patted the kudu because there seemed to be enough wonder there to last me a lifetime.

Eventually, I drifted off to sleep with mighty Victoria Falls rumbling beneath us. Somewhere in the jungle not too far away, Shirley was also sleeping, and I wondered if his belly was full.

A simian side of me hoped it was.

David and I at The Rocks.
Harare, Zimbabwe. 1996.

Vervet Monkey (*Chlorocebus pygerythrus*).
Habitat: Savanna, forest and woodlands. Range: Southern Africa.

Chapter Eleven

Kamau
(1998)

Two years later, Dee and I were back in East Africa on an overland trip that began in Nairobi, Kenya. We would meander throughout East Africa for several months before arriving at our final destination, Dar es Salaam, Tanzania.

We were there during the dry season. A heatwave had ravaged Nairobi for weeks, and the hotels only occasionally had water for showers. I took this as a blow because even in the best of times, Nairobi can be a challenging city to experience, and we didn't need anything else working against us.

The streets of Nairobi—Nairobbery, the travelers called it— were populated by gangs of con artists. If you watched a typical boulevard for an hour, you would soon realize that a dozen grifters were coordinating their efforts, even though they were dressed differently. A few looked like college kids, others wore beggar's vestments, and several men were in business suits.

They created scenes—scams—that drew in the unwary. Sometimes, one of them pretended to be a student that had fallen on hard times, or a refugee from Somalia that desperately needed help. And I've heard of other cases where they claimed to be frantically waiting for a bank transfer or for money to help their family escape the clutches of evil men.

All were scams.

It was tough not to fall prey to these guys. They would often begin by having a violent or sketchy gang member confront you, and then the man in the business suit would come to your supposed rescue.

I watched them for hours from cafés, feeling like I was a naturalist documenting their movements. When they grouped, I tried to pick out which one was the alpha — who was in charge.

I expected the leader to be the one wearing a suit, but that wasn't always the case. But despite the different clothing, one of them always had a bit of a power walk.

Plus, simian motives seemed to be at play here. Don't let anyone fool you: When humans get aggressive, it is usually about territory, food or females. Any other motive — even money — is just a front.

Money, after all, will buy those things.

There were a lot of pickpockets and thieves, too, who mingled with the fast-walking crowds on the city's busy street. Set down your pack, or leave something on a bus seat, and it'd be gone in a second.

And maybe I shouldn't generalize so much. Kenya is still a developing country, and by comparison, I was richer than most of the people I passed on the sidewalk. Instead of calling them thieves, maybe I should call them desperate people looking for an opportunity.

Either way, I could not afford to lose the modest amount of money I had, so I kept my eyes peeled and my possessions close.

At the time, I was reading a book on the behavior of a troop of baboons and felt much of the discussion could have applied to these street gangs. They existed in complex social groups, had what might be called organized hunts, and they related to each other through a hierarchical system with an alpha male at the top.

I hope I'm not offending anyone when I compare humans to other primates, but I've found wherever I am in the world, that's just what I do. Caring, thoughtful people remind me of orangutans.

When I see playful humans, I recall gibbons. Watchful or nosey humans bring back my memories of the sentinel langurs.

I should add that the reverse is also true. Often while I am watching primates, they remind me of people, most likely because I witness not just signs of intelligence but also individuals with personalities and very recognizable emotions.

Often, they make me think of different people I have known.

Teenage boys can be very much like baboons, and so could the chiselers that worked the streets. Every time we were changing money at the bank, there was a whole show developing while we were getting back to the taxi that was waiting by the bank door.

Always, some nice man ran up to us, acting like he had something important to say, trying to stop us from entering the taxi.

If you don't want to be ripped off, you do not stop. Never.

At night, the sweltering heat would let up. But the memory of it stayed with me for a few hours into the evening, as if the now-departed sun was some famished desert demon who still watched me from the shadows.

I enjoyed walking the streets at night. There were far fewer people out, resulting in fewer scam crews. The police knew most of the players, and without the crowds, they had nowhere to hide. The Nairobi cops, who were really tough, would shake down thieves as readily as the thieves stole from the tourists.

But you didn't want to drift too close to any dark alleys, or you might get yourself mugged.

Even though Dee and I were married by then, and I had plenty of other things to occupy my mind while traveling, I still suffered from pithecophilia. Theories about apes still bounced around my head as if they had the run of the place.

What tended to hold my attention at the time was the perspective through which apes viewed their lives. I accepted that as humans, we had a well-developed part of the brain that was used to think about ourselves—the default brain network—but I couldn't wrap my brain around how a mind would work without it—a mind where the "I" or "ego" was less present.

How would that affect motivation or even free will?

And no amount of cogitating seemed to make these questions any clearer to me, so I decided to study humans for a while instead of primates.

I experimented by taking Dee to a bar that had the potential to be a dangerous place, but I felt would be safe for us if we followed a few rules that had been set down in the book on baboons: We would stay in positive circles of behavior and avoid displaced aggression.

In other words, we would try not to get into trouble.

The establishment in question was called the Modern Green Bar, and I decided we should visit it during the final hours before it closed, late in the evening.

The bar was located off Latima Road, on River Road, where the buildings were dilapidated, and the city streets narrowed. The lanes were lined with shops, all of which had metal grates pulled down at this time of night and were locked up tightly.

We left our room at 12:30 a.m. to walk there.

Before we left, I had instructed Dee to wear only a worn pair of jeans, a T-shirt, and sandals. No jewelry or money belt or anything glittery that might attract predators—or in this case, thieves.

I had five dollars' worth of Kenyan shillings in my pocket and nothing else.

"So why are we going out with almost no cash and dressed like this?" asked Dee.

I stopped and said, "Everybody makes a lot of fuss about the thieves in Nairobi, but I wanted to show you that when you're not an intended target, the people here can be quite nice."

In my mind I pictured Shirley the baboon, who'd left us alone the instant he determined we had no food.

I supposed I should have been fearful of being assaulted, but I was rarely scared when I traveled Africa for some unknown reason.

We strolled the quiet backstreets with the city sleeping around us. Stray cats and mangy-looking dogs scurried about. In one alley, the red-glowing tip of a cigarette glared at me from the darkness, but its owner stayed put as we passed.

Only when we approached the Modern Green Bar did we begin to hear signs of life — music and shouting.

The bar was the only place open in the entire neighborhood. In fact, it might have been the only bar open in the city, which is why it always filled in the late hours.

It had an infamous reputation.

This was the place for Nairobi's last call. Here the city's bartenders and wait staff assembled after their own establishments had closed for the night.

This was the place the prostitutes went when they'd had no luck finding a client elsewhere. And it's where the thieves whose failed efforts to bear fruit had also gravitated.

I suppose it was where the successful thieves went to celebrate after a successful con, too.

From the street, it looked like the kind of place to end an evening— it didn't strike me as a 'starter' bar. The adjective that was often used to describe the clientele was nefarious.

We had napped in the late afternoon. And now, around 1:00 a.m., we were both wide awake as we navigated the pothole-ridden sidewalks.

The air was dead-still, without a trace of a breeze.

A queue had formed outside the open door of the Modern Green Bar, and a line of men stood and patiently waited, swaying like sleeping elephants. A quick glance told me these were low-ranking males. If they'd been baboons, a few frustrated individuals would have been sneaking off to masturbate in the bushes.

A glimpse within revealed a dense cloud of folks shouting, drinking and laughing. There were no white people inside.

"So, what's so special about this place?" asked Dee.

I grinned, "Nothing, it's just open late."

She peered inside. "Looks a little sketchy."

I smiled again. I wanted to tell her that with primates, the first thing to do if someone offends you is scream like hell, but instead I only said, "We'll be fine."

A large black man sat on a wooden stool by the entrance. He was the bouncer, and he gripped a thick staff, about three inches wide and four feet long. His skin-tight black T-shirt bulged from a muscular chest and biceps, and he looked stern as he eyeballed each person in line.

I later learned the man's name was Kamau, a Swahili word meaning Quiet Warrior, and I thought it an apt name. I could tell he could handle himself. He wasn't resting on his laurels, maintaining his position with sheer psychological intimidation.

I was glad I had no reason to challenge him for the alpha position.

We headed for the end of the line, but Kamau motioned with his head for us to come forward. He looked us up and down, and then chuckled to himself and let us in.

I smiled at him, glad for the support of a dominant male.

A few of the locals grumbled when we stepped in front of the line, but a stern look from the bouncer quickly silenced their protests.

A wave of heat, heavy with the stench of sweat, hit us as we entered the avocado-green rectangular room. The floor was sticky with spilled beer. All the tables were occupied, and most of the patrons were standing.

Along the back wall a mesh wire cage contained the bartender. Warm beer could be purchased through a small window in front of him.

I saw a few familiar faces in the crowd and knew I had observed them on the street fleecing passersby. I felt quite a few eyes on us.

In less than a minute, we were both covered with sweat. The only circulation in the place was a large ceiling fan. Its blades thick with dust and cobwebs that seemed to only make things worse by slowly stirring the late-night cocktail of sweat, beer and urine.

An African song with a wild, crazy beat pounded through ancient speakers. Most of the people around us were recklessly drunk. The rhythm of the metal drums had them swaying like a grove of bamboo on a windy day.

We found a spot along a sidewall and leaned against each other while we watched a toothless old man in a white cap move his hips rudely and slap his ass like he was riding a horse. His inebriated friends cheered him on, and one handed him a fresh beer when he stopped.

Dee looked sideways at me. "You sure know how to show a girl a good time."

I had to laugh. It was quite a show. I settled back and studied the behavior of the bar's clientele, noting who was fighting with whom, observing people in the crowd engage in trysts, friendships and alliances.

A few prostitutes shared the sidewall with us. They looked bored, standing there in short skirts, resigned that the remainder of the night held little promise.

Dee scanned the room and looked at me. "How about a drink?"

I held up a finger. "Give me a minute."

I left our spot by the wall, made my way through the throng, and approached the cage. As I handed the bartender a few shillings, I glimpsed a small refrigerator on the floor.

I paused. "Got any cold ones?"

He ignored me. Clearly, he wished he was the alpha and not stuck in the cage. I figured he had settled for more money instead of the more powerful position of bouncer.

I added a few more shillings, and he bent down and grabbed two cool Tuskers from the fridge.

"*Asante sana*," I said, which is thank you very much in Swahili.

He grunted and turned away.

Over the next hour, Dee and I watched the crowd.

A few men walked by and casually scanned our clothing. I could see them determine that we had nothing of value and moved on.

The prostitutes had eyed me initially, but once they saw Dee, their eyes drifted on. We were very much in love, and apparently, that was obvious. A few exchanged smiles with Dee.

If I had been with another man, we might have been drawn into a fight, or if Dee had been there alone or with a girlfriend, I'm sure she would have had to fend off some unwanted attention.

But in our current sociobiological condition, no one messed with us.

And it was refreshing to watch the crowd and feel we were accepted.

Now that we weren't considered a mark, the thieves forgot about us and abandoned their designs. It was strange to see some of them smile. We had literally entered a den of thieves, but they now had other things on their minds — like having fun.

I felt like I was seeing them for the first time.

It reminded me of a friend whom I used to see in bars in New Hampshire. He was male, my age, and we would talk until he noticed a girl he fancied in the crowd — from then on out, even though he'd continue chatting, I could tell his mind was elsewhere.

He was worthless in conversation if there was a pretty girl within twenty feet. But when there were no women around, I enjoyed his company.

That's how I felt now. By showing up with nothing of value — and being in love, I suppose — we had cleared away the elements that may have drawn us into a conflict.

Initially, I had compared the people of the bar with baboons, but then I remembered my experiences with Shirley and changed my mind. Baboons were fierce and often dangerous.

In this case, the way the alcohol had mellowed the crowd made them seem more like macaques.

I remembered the Rhesus monkeys that would routinely overtake the New Nepali Friendly Café in southern Nepal. There had been such a sense of family in the troop. If you watched them for an hour, you witnessed so many interactions — playing, grooming, fighting — just like in this bar.

I loved it, and I felt like these were my kind of people.

Everyone was celebrating life in their own way. And they didn't seem to mind that we were there - celebrating with them.

Later, things did get out of hand. The drunks turned baboonish. I watched two men pound on the back of a man who was choking, while to their left, two other men tussled and were grabbing each other's collars.

The fighting men had my attention because I didn't want their violence to spill our way. With baboons, when one is insulted by a more powerful male and direct retaliation is too dangerous, the first thought is to find someone else to pay for it. This is the kind of displaced aggression that trickles down through the tribe.

Kamau had moved his stool inside the bar and now sat in the doorway. When he noticed the fighting men, he slammed the base of his staff on the cement floor. The vibration stopped the two fighters instantly as if the staff contained the power to immediately suck all the alcohol and adrenaline out of them.

Both men looked at the bouncer and began making appeasement gestures, holding their arms extended with the palms up. Male baboons that want to show they like another male will yank on the others' penis a few times — fortunately, there was none of that.

The bouncer nodded at me, and for the first time that evening, I saw him grin.

I grinned back.

And later, when we left, I stopped by his stool and shook his hand.

As we walked away, he asked where our hotel was.

I told him, and he nodded to a man leaning against the wall.

"This man will escort you," said Kamau. "There are dangers in the night."

I realized the merit of his offer and nodded thanks. The bar was clearing out, and there were now a lot of people in the street.

The man leaning against the wall joined us, and he started off when I told him the name of our hotel.

"Goodnight, my friends," yelled Kamau as he turned back to the bar.

That was our first of several encounters with the Modern Green clientele. During our late-night jaunts in Nairobi, I learned a valuable lesson...

It's always good to have an alpha like Kamau on your side.

Hanging out with a friend
in Arusha, Tanzania. 1998.

Bonobo (*Pan paniscus*).
Habitat: Lowland rainforest. Range: Congo basin, Central Africa.

Chapter Twelve

River Horses
(1998)

We left Nairobi. The drought drove us out and we headed northwest for Lake Naivasha. The lake is located in the Great Rift Valley at 6,181 feet, where it is much cooler than the city because of the altitude. The surrounding forests are home to hundreds of species of birds, and the lake supports a large population of hippos.

We stayed at Fisherman's Camp, on the shore of the lake. Thick-trunked acacia trees rose into a beautifully intertwined canopy over the campground. The upper branches were alive with bird calls when we arrived. In the shrubs around our tent, small African parrots called Lovebirds chattered playfully.

I smiled as my eyes drifted over the setting, pleased with my plan. With a little luck, I would soon introduce my wife to one of Africa's most magical scenes.

The camping area where we stayed was separated from the lake by an earthen wall, about ten feet tall and just as wide, and fifty feet long. On the far side of the wall, a grass lawn extended for a hundred feet to the lakeshore.

The grass looked like it had recently been mowed, but I knew it was cropped instead by hippos that left the lake each night to graze—thus, the earthen wall to keep the campers separated from the hippos.

I'd been in this campsite a few years earlier, before the earthen divider had been created, and when someone spooked a hippo one night, it charged so closely past my tent that it ripped out a corner stake and guyline.

I clearly remembered the ground shaking as the beast approached. The sense of helplessness I felt was overwhelming. I knew the hippo wasn't charging me; my tent was simply between it and the safety of the lake. But that thought helped little.

In my panic, I anticipated the impact of a ton of muscle moving at nearly twenty miles per hour. There's a reason hippos account for more deaths than lions.

Needless to say, that wasn't the story I told Dee. After all, I was organizing a romantic outing—watching hippos graze under the moonlight.

When the sun began to dip in the west, we walked along the lakeshore, watching fish eagles swoop low and pick off their prey. Marabou storks gazed at us, motionlessly, only their eyes following our passage.

I heard a troop of black and white colobus monkeys (*Colobus guereza*) making a ruckus in the trees that lined the shore, but I could not catch a glimpse of them.

The campground had a few rowboats moored to a small dock, and we took one out. I kept us fairly close to the shore for a few reasons.

First, there are lots of hippos out here, and they can be quite dangerous. Hippos live in groups of five to thirty cows and young, and there's always a large bull presiding over them.

And bulls can be cranky.

During the day, the group stays cool by remaining in the water, resting. While you might not even see a bull, he's there.

Venture too far into his territory, and suddenly it looks like somebody fired a torpedo, with a ripple coming at you from across the water—and then it's time to paddle like hell.

The other reason I didn't go far into the lake was because of the sudden storms that sometimes arise. The Maasai knew about them and named the lake *Nai'posha*, which means "rough water."

I had learned that lesson the hard way on my last visit.

After spending a week climbing Mount Kenya back then, I stumbled upon Fisherman's Camp for a little R & R. My climbing friend and I hadn't realized we were coming out of the mountains on Easter Sunday.

We arrived without any food or any cash to buy a meal. It was Sunday, so the bank in town was closed, and we couldn't cash a traveler's check.

The campground was thick with the aroma of food being cooked, and this was making my stomach growl uncontrollably. I resigned myself to a hungry night, with plans to get money and a meal first thing in the morning.

Until then, we decided to go for a rowboat ride to try to escape the mouth-watering smells.

But thirty minutes into the excursion, a massive black cloud bore down on us as if drawn magnetically to our boat. I turned the craft around and began rowing as hard as I could.

Moments before the rain hit us, I somehow knocked a large-mouth black bass into the rowboat with the backstroke of an oar.

It was almost a foot-and-a-half long and must have weighed four pounds. It was the largest freshwater fish I ever caught. I was barely comprehending what had happened when the clouds unloaded a torrent of water, and I jumped back on the oars.

When we got back to the campsite, drenched, I showed my catch and told my tale, and the news spread through the campground. And while we grilled our fish over an open fire, numerous other campers stopped by and donated vegetables, bread and salad to complete the meal.

The manager of the campground was a god-fearing Christian. When Dee and I checked in this time around, I mentioned the event, and he smiled and nodded. He laughed and said he still remembered when God had provided a meal for a hungry boy on an Easter Sunday.

Dee and I ventured a little further into the lake, marveling at the Aberdare Mountains as they rose behind us.

I kept an eye on a group of hippos nestled in a papyrus thicket a little further along the shore — maybe a hundred and fifty feet away.

I was afraid of them but also drawn to them.

A group of hippos is called a bloat, and I glanced at the bloat by the shore. A dozen heads watched me, ears waggling, nostrils blowing.

I shouted their Swahili name, "Kiboko!" and a few large females snorted back.

As a kid, I had seen my first hippo at a Barnum & Bailey Circus.

The poor creature had been in a tank, under a red light, with a banner dangling above that read: Blood-sweating hippopotamus.

I know now that what had covered the hippo was neither sweat nor blood but a natural sunscreen that turns red-orange soon after being secreted.

When traveling in Africa, I still told folks my name was Kiboko.

I may not have understood the mind of a hippo, but I loved their fierce independence.

The males can be dangerous and unpredictable, but their disposition is driven by an instinct to protect their family and territory. And when a hippo — the third largest animal in Africa — perks up and lets you know you are trespassing, it's smart to listen. They are quite formidable.

Zulu warriors shout, "He is better than a lion — he is a hippopotamus" because they know the lion is no match for a hippo.

We returned to the dock without incident; and then went back to our tent to douse ourselves in bug spray and change into long pants and boots, something we always did before nightfall as protection against mosquitoes.

I've known far more travelers hospitalized for dengue fever or malaria than those injured by large animals.

The moon was a few days past full and waning. It rose after we had gone to bed. But the bright, spectral shadows it cast on our tent left no doubt of its presence. Around midnight I shook Dee awake and we got dressed.

We exited our tent and silently climbed the earthen wall. Soon we were peering over the top to see a dozen hippos grazing placidly down below.

The moonlight bathed the lawn, trees, hippos and us, in a magical light. Beyond the hippos, the lake glittered in the distance.

A large bull moved just below the wall. The moonlight glowed on his barrel-shaped torso. He was of good size; I would guess about five thousand pounds. I knew there were exceptional bulls that weighed seven and even over nine thousand pounds, but I bit my tongue and kept the nerdy animal facts to myself for once.

It was enough to observe these behemoths as they calmly grazed, fully exposed and at ease.

I silently laid out a blanket.

We sat and peered down at the hippo, only yards away.

The bull was unaware of us and was simply yawning when he opened his mouth impossibly wide, exposing a pink mouth full of jagged ivory teeth.

But my heart almost skidded to a stop when he did.

Dee stiffened next to me, then softened when the hippo moved on.

I whispered to her, "The canines and incisors can grow to over a foot long—but those teeth play no role in feeding and are only used in combat."

She rolled her eyes at me, and I clamped my mouth shut.

But the facts continued bouncing around my head, pausing at times on the tip of my tongue. Hippos have a bite force of nearly two thousand pounds per square inch. They can consume a hundred and fifty pounds of grass in a single night. When they grind their teeth, they are actually sharpening them.

And so on.

I took off my daypack, which I had loaded with picnic supplies.

Soon I had some Raka cheese cut into slices, and a few pieces of Mandazi fry bread set out, as well as a pile of passion fruit and a single ripe mango.

"Looks like somebody has a plan," said Dee.

I laughed and nodded, "Yup, I'm always dragging you up mountains or into desert canyons, and I thought we might do something more serene."

It was more than that. One of the biggest differences between Dee and me is the way we each experience the moment. I'm rarely there, and instead, I am busy remembering the past or imagining the future.

Dee tends to embrace the present moment. She seems more at home with what is currently going on.

But we both enjoy watching wildlife, and I had hoped we might be on the same page for a while observing hippos.

I smiled at her, and she tilted her head back to bask in the moonlight, her body swaying to the gentle breeze that flowed over our hill.

Dee let her eyes drift over the creatures, and we observed them prune the grass with their broad horny lips. The evening was warm, awash in a pleasant silver glimmer.

"Well, this is romantic," she said. "Although they look and sound a little like giant pigs."

In a rush, I said, "Their name means river horse in ancient Greek, but even though they resemble even-toed ungulates like pigs, they're more closely related to whales, dolphins and porpoises."

She gave me an amused look, and I added, "From which they diverged about fifty-five million years ago."

A mischievous grin swept over Dee's face as she let the random facts settle, and then asked, "Are you sure this isn't all just a set up for you to talk about the amorous bonobos?"

I sighed and shook my head. This was one of Dee's favorite subjects to tease me about.

Bonobos (*Pan paniscus*), also known as pygmy chimpanzees, are an IUCN 'endangered' ape that lives in a 190,000 square mile area of the Congo Basin in the Democratic Republic of Congo. Data on their population numbers is sparse, but it is estimated that there are between thirty and fifty thousand individuals.

They are one of two species in the genus *Pan*; the common chimpanzee is the other. Together, they are the closest living relatives to humans.

Although bonobos and chimpanzees are very similar, the ancestral species were subdivided when the Congo River formed and cut through the land it inhabited. Almost two million years of isolation resulted in bonobos and chimpanzees evolving into different species. As expected, they also evolved unique behaviors.

Bonobos are matriarchal; an older female leads each troop. Bonobo females are promiscuous and have sexual interactions more frequently than any other primate. In fact, it appears that sexual activity plays a significant part in the lives of bonobos, and it is often used as a means of conflict resolution.

Promiscuous behavior ripples through the troop in interesting ways. Because of this, it results in far less aggressive encounters between males and females. Because males cannot be sure which offspring are theirs, they leave the infants and juveniles alone, while Chimpanzees sometimes kill young that they don't deem their descendants.

The common chimpanzee is quite different from the Bonobo. Chimps patrol their territories, and when they come upon a neighboring solo male, they often kill him. In contrast, bonobos seem to prefer sexual contact over violent confrontation with outsiders.

And this is where I would get in trouble with Dee.

She looked over the picnic and said, "So if we were bonobos, this display of food might lead to sex, correct?"

I nodded my head hesitantly. "Maybe. I guess."

I'd made the mistake of telling Dee that there had been documented accounts of troops of bonobos coming upon a tree that was particularly ripe with fruit, and suddenly everyone — male, female, young and old — fell into a group genital-rubbing session.

Apparently, the sex reduced tension.

Dee glanced at the mango and shrugged. "Well, I'm not promising anything — I don't care how nice of a spread you set out."

I laughed. "Okay, no pressure."

"Come over here and give me a bonobo kiss," said Dee, and I leaned forward and brushed her lips with mine, and at last minute our tongues touched lightly.

Bonobos have been observed engaging in tongue kissing — the only non-human animal ever witnessed doing so. There was a part of me that filled with pride at the idea that my wife knew that fact.

I picked up the mango, sliced it down the middle and took out the seed, and then cut grid marks into it before presenting half to Dee.

The bull hippo had moved away, but two cows were now grazing at the base of the hill below us.

While she took a bite, I thought more about bonobos, who are the only primates that engage in face-to-face missionary-positioned sex. But I kept my mouth shut.

I had read about a tourist who photographed two western gorillas having face-to-face-sex, but I decided that fact was somehow unromantic as well. So, I kept that factoid under my hat too.

Instead, I sat there silently, watching the hippos drift under the skeletal shadows cast by the stately acacia trees. I tried my best to simply be there, feeling the light breeze under the moonlight.

And when Dee lightly leaned against me, a surge of warmth flowed through my body, and I felt lucky to be in love, in Africa, and under the moon and stars.

Hippo (in Swahili, *Kiboko*)
at Lake Naivasha, Kenya.

Eastern Black and White Colobus (*Colobus guereza*).
Habitat: Lowland tropical rainforest. Range: Equatorial Africa.

Chapter Thirteen

Elsamere
(1998)

A few days later, we rowed about a mile and a half along the lake shoreline to the former home of George and Joy Adamson — a place called Elsamere. I was at the oars, facing backward, and Dee sat perched on the small bow seat, her face lit up in the morning sun as she scanned the water ahead of us.

We spied one bloat of hippos deeper in the lake. Their grunts sounded eerily close due to how sound travels easily across open water, but thankfully none appeared before us.

The cobalt blue sky expanded above. The clouds were racing by, but there was hardly a breeze at water level, and the boat moved effortlessly with each stroke.

Dee reclined against the side of the boat and adjusted her sunglasses.

A pied kingfisher skimmed along beside us.

A goliath heron eyed us from the shore.

I sculled along, my mind running through what I knew about the founders of Elsamere.

Joy Adamson was a naturalist, artist, and author, who came to Africa in 1937 when she was twenty-seven. Her first husband, Peter

Bally, a botanist, encouraged Joy to paint and sketch Kenya's flora and fauna. Their marriage was short-lived. In the 1940s, while on safari, she met senior wildlife warden George Adamson. By 1944, they were married.

Her book, *Born Free* — and the Academy Award-winning movie that followed — projected her into the international spotlight in the 1960s. It was near the end of that decade that I learned about her conservation efforts associated with a lioness named Elsa.

I remember watching the movie for the first time like it was yesterday. In all the other shows on Africa that I viewed, the animals were dangerous and unpredictable. But in *Born Free,* they were portrayed as affectionate. The movie revealed both the tender way the Adamson's cared for the young lioness named Elsa, and the love Elsa showed for her caretakers.

Even now, merely thinking about *Born Free* makes me want to help an animal.

The theme song that won an Oscar continuously visits me, as does the perspective I gained from the film. The bond between Joy and Elsa had been clear to me as an eight-year-old.

It was the first time I imagined animals capable of loving on such a grand scale — equal to our ability to love.

The movie retells a story that began in 1956 when George Adamson shot a charging lioness. When examining her body, he noticed that she was lactating and surmised that she had most likely been defending her cubs. A short search revealed three of them hidden in a rocky crevasse.

Realizing they would die on their own, George brought the cubs home. The Adamsons decided to raise the smallest of the cubs, whom they named Elsa, but as she grew, they eventually chose to set her free.

The problem was the young lioness did not know how to survive on her own. They spent months training her to hunt, and released her into the wild for short periods of time.

In her books, *Born Free, Living Free,* and *Forever Free,* Joy Adamson described their efforts to return Elsa to the wild.

Not only were they successful, but when they located Elsa a year after her release, they discovered she had her own litter of cubs by her side. This was the first time a released lion had been documented to reproduce. Joy Adamson also rehabilitated a cheetah and a leopard, but she is mostly known for Elsa's story.

As a kid, I thought of Elsa almost every time the lions at Capron Park coughed a greeting. But now, I also reflected on the experiences I'd personally had with big cats, and those were much scarier.

Over the years, I've spent hundreds of hours watching lions, leopards and cheetahs in Africa. The skill and ferociousness of their kills was an awesome spectacle to witness. Once a lion has sunk its claws and canines into the prey, a battle ensues that is both tough to observe and impossible to turn away from.

And if the rest of the pride catches up, it's unnerving to watch them overtake the struggling animal until it almost completely disappears in a mass of lions.

In most of these instances, I watched from the safety of a vehicle. Maybe that's why when I encountered big cats on foot, it scared me so much.

That time I was lost in Sumatra, and on other walking safaris in Asia, came immediately to mind. Although I never saw a tiger, I felt like I had sensed them around me – perhaps it was just my nerves, but it left me terrified.

And then there was the lioness that stepped into my tent a few years back. Having witnessed lionesses on the hunt, I knew what they were capable of. I've seen a lioness nearly rip a warthog in half in a frenetic attack.

I feared them all. Even thinking about it made the hair on my arms stand on end.

Would I ever get back to that world in which I yearned to bond with a big cat? It seemed to me that when I was around them, I still vacillated between terror and fascination.

I would find out soon, I thought, as we headed to Elsamere.

I heard the theme song for *Born Free* whispering softly on the wind as we approached Elsamere in our boat. It was like my eight-year-old self had awakened from a nap. The gentle breeze blew us directly toward a small dock as if guided by a magical hand.

A few primates called out from the tall trees lining the shore.

I figured they were probably colobus monkeys that reputedly lived there. While Sub-Saharan Africa is home to five species of colobus monkeys, I knew that black and white colobus had long ago taken residence in the trees surrounding the Adamson estate.

As I prepared to grab the dock and tie off, I scanned the canopy, hoping to see one.

They are beautiful creatures with bushy tails and black faces surrounded by white fur. A glossy black coat covers their limbs and trunk, and a U-shaped mantle of long white hair falls on their backs.

In the primate world, colobus monkeys are known for their proclivity for being rather listless. Typically, they live near their food source, so little time is needed for foraging. Their troops are typically eight to fifteen individuals, which seems to be enough to expend some lookouts to spot danger but is not sufficient to deplete the food source. They are patriarchal, led by a male, but overall, they display low aggression within their own troop.

They know how to chill.

When we stood on the dock, I managed to make out a colobus high up in the trees. Males can grow up to thirty pounds, and this one was an impressive size. I could see his long body splayed across a limb, not a care in the world, like he was two hours into a visit to an opium den.

We tied off the boat and followed a stone path to a large cottage with a reception area. Elsamere sat on lovely grounds with stately acacia trees. There was also a small museum dedicated to the Adamsons, and a garden area with tables where you could take refreshments.

I heard sometimes they played a movie for guests and was pleased to see one was scheduled in about an hour. Until then, we were led to an outside table in the garden where we were served tea.

There were so many birds in the trees that it seemed like a migration was underway. It appeared that the birds were as excited to be at the Adamson's home as I was.

From our table, I could occasionally hear the monkeys over the cacophony of the birds, but I could not see them at all. While Dee wrote a postcard to her mom, I strolled through the gardens and eventually sighted a dozen colobuses, high in the canopy, all of them draped over the branches.

It could be their laid-back rhythm allows them to live longer. In the wild, they can survive twenty years; macaques live fifteen, and Vervet monkeys only twelve.

It's no wonder they liked the protected area of Elsamere. The high-density forest seems to be the ideal habitat for a colobus monkey. There's plenty of acacia leaves, flowers and fruits to forage, and it was largely free of predators.

In the wild, it seems everyone takes advantage of the colobuses´ lackadaisical nature. Eagles pick them off from the canopy as they nap during the day, leopards stalk them by night, and chimpanzees hunt them ruthlessly.

Of course, the main predator is man, who not only hunts them for meat but also destroys their habitat. But at Elsamere, for nearly fifty years now, they have a refuge.

I returned to Dee and sipped my tea until we were called for the movie, which turned out to be more about George Adamson than about Joy or Elsa the lion.

George Adamson was born in Etawah, India, in 1906, was educated in England, and came to Africa when he was eighteen. When he arrived in Kenya, he began working on his father's coffee plantation but later tried his hand at various jobs, including safari hunter and prospector.

In 1938 he joined Kenya's wildlife department. Eventually, he became the Senior Wildlife Warden for the Northern Frontier District. His African friends called him *Baba ya Simba*, "Father of Lions" in Swahili.

And he was about to become one of my heroes.

I thought I knew his story from the movie *Born Free*, in which Bill Travers plays his part, but when I watched the home movie at Elsamere, I discovered how much I did not know about him.

In 1961 Adamson retired as a wildlife warden and began rehabilitating lions who could not care for themselves in the wild because they had been orphaned, injured, or had spent time in captivity. For the rest of his life, nearly twenty-eight years, he put all his time and energy into working with these big cats, eventually reintroducing them into the wild.

In 1970 he established a camp at Kora National Reserve in northern Kenya, and from there, helped numerous lions.

I knew none of this before my trip to Elsamere.

One of the museum staff dimmed the lights, and an old 8mm projector began ticking away. In the opening scene, a shirtless man in his sixties hops out of a Land Rover and walks toward the camera. He has a mop of white hair, all of it combed back and falling on his shoulders. His facial hair is white too. He has bushy eyebrows, a white mustache, and a goatee in need of a trim.

His skin is tanned and leathery, but his eyes are alert and sensitive. I found myself enchanted by this character as I watched him confidently stroll forward.

He smiled at the camera and seemed surprised when suddenly, a four-hundred-pound male lion tackles him from the side. They roll to the ground, and I gasp, feeling like I'm watching him being mauled. Suddenly, the two flop onto their backs, and I could see George laughing.

The man sat up and scratched the lion's belly and then hugged him.

The lion, in return, rolled upright and rubbed his head against George's chest, almost knocking him on his back again.

It was clear these two creatures were friends.

I knew George helped raise a lioness named Elsa, but who was this guy?

The film passed through a montage of images of George and various lions over the span of several decades. In most of the scenes, he was in shorts and shirtless, although sometimes he sported a short-sleeved, button-up khaki shirt. In some he was smoking a pipe.

He was depicted repairing vehicles, napping, or surveying the land. But in all these images, lions were close at hand. A few of them were cubs, but most were grown—several were quite large with thick manes.

In one picture, George walked into the sunset on the plain with a large male lion by his side. In another, he was driving a Land Rover with a lion perched on the top of the cab, and in still another, he was peering through the bush at a herd of Thompson's gazelles with a lion, who was also watching the game intently.

My favorite images were those from campsites where George slept next to a lion, who had his tremendous forearm resting on his human friend's body.

There was no doubt that he was friends with these lions. I'm terrified of lions, but I don't think I would be if George Adamson were with me. The love and respect he showed his lions brought out qualities that many didn't know existed. His observations revealed that lions were capable of feelings, trust, and lasting friendships with humans.

Lions are not just killing machines.

Adamson published his experiences with big cats. Two of his books— *Lifetime with Lions* and *My Pride and Joy* — were instrumental in showing the world that lions could be rehabilitated after captivity and were capable of a far wider range of behavior than was previously known.

In the 1987 edition of Joy Adamson's *Born Free*, naturalist George Schaller wrote, "The Adamsons gave us truths about the species that cannot be found in a biologist's notebook. Their efforts at reintroduction and rehabilitation taught the scientific community invaluable lessons."

The movie ended and we drifted back to the garden. The birds had quieted down, and in the new silence, we could hear the colobus monkeys calling to each other from the canopy.

A group of hippos lingered by the dock, so we decided to wait and have another pot of tea until they moved on.

In the canopy, about thirty feet above us, a dozen colobus monkeys slowly moved by. I glimpsed at several females with young clinging to them and remembered that they practiced allomothering. This is when females not closely related to a juvenile assist with its upbringing by providing food, carrying it, and protecting it against predators.

This is common among many primates, including Vervets, squirrel monkeys and macaques. I imagine it was also a trait possessed by our early hominin ancestors because modern humans practice allomothering as well.

We sipped our tea quietly, watching the colobus, and my thoughts returned to the Adamsons again. Although their legacy of conservation continues at Elsamere, both Joy and George have long been deceased. Like Dian Fossey and so many other noble conservationists, they were both slain — one by poachers, the other by a disgruntled former employee.

Joy was killed shortly before her 70th birthday while on safari in the Shaba National Reserve. It was initially believed a lion had killed her, but an investigation later determined her wounds were inflicted by a knife, not a large predator's canines and claws.

Her beautiful lioness, Elsa, died of a tick-borne disease called babesiosis. George located Elsa in the final weeks of her life and stayed with her to the end. She died with her head in his lap. Elsa and Joy are buried next to each other in Meru National Park.

George was murdered nine years later, in 1989.

His death was a tragedy, and yet somehow befitting his adventurous life. While at his camp in the Kora National Park, George received a distress call about armed poachers having pinned down one of his assistants and a young European tourist.

He rushed to their aid, fought off the assailants, and rescued the pair. In the scuffle, he was fatally wounded.

George was eighty-three years old when he died.

He is buried in the park, next to his brother and three of his favorite lions: Boy, Super Cub and Mugie.

I mourned the death of the Adamsons and others like Dian Fossey, but I also knew that thousands of men and women had lost their lives trying to protect animals in the last twenty years.

Each year millions of individual animals and thousands of species are hunted or trapped by poachers. If it weren't for these unsung heroes who gave their lives to protect animals like rhinos, elephants and tigers — along with many lesser-known creatures — many might already be extinct.

As it stands, wildlife populations have declined by 70% globally over the last fifty years. A few minutes of research on this subject is enough to depress anyone.

I sat in the pleasant garden silently, thinking about the Adamsons. As a boy, I never contemplated their deaths. They weighed heavily on me now, as did the deaths of the other park rangers and conservationists.

Dee must have noticed the sadness that had come over me because she started questioning me about the colobus monkeys.

"So, what's so special about these guys?" she asked with a nod at the canopy. Dee usually knew better than to ask me about primates, so I must have looked grim.

I glanced up and gave a weak smile.

"Well, we don't have much of a chance to see the behavior I'd really like to see," I said.

Her brow furrowed slightly. "Why's that?"

I scanned the other trees around us. "When a group of colobuses are reunited with an extended family group, they participate in a greeting ritual. I think the chances of us being here when another troop happens to pass by is pretty slim."

Now Dee cast her gaze around.

I continued, "Generally, greeting behavior is carried out by the approaching monkey, and it doesn't seem to have anything to do with mating or courting."

Dee stared at me, waiting. "What exactly do they do?"

I managed a smile. "There are several variations, but basically they just grasp their fellow colobus by the shoulders, and then pull them in for a hug."

Her face lit up. "That's so sweet!"

A short laugh escaped my lungs. "Yeah, I suppose it is."

A giant kingfisher fluttered down and hopped around on the table next to us. We watched it silently.

Ten minutes later, we stood to leave. The hippos had moved on, and we were both eager to return to Fisherman's Camp.

I was about to walk toward the dock when Dee stepped in front of me, put both hands on my shoulder, and pulled me in for a hug.

At first, I chuckled, feeling like she was humoring me, but then her warmth radiated through my body, and I hugged her back. She was of my tribe—maybe the hug was reaffirming that just like a colobus hug—and suddenly, the world was bright again.

Lion in Kenya's Maasai Mara
Game Reserve. 1998.

With my father, Ron, at The Explorers Club Headquarters.
New York City, NY. 1999.

Chapter Fourteen

The Explorers Club
(1999)

*I*n the summer of 1998, Dee and I camped on the Stampede Trail, located a few miles from the town of Healy, Alaska. Further down the trail was the abandoned bus in which Christopher McCandless had died seven years before. Neither the book about his misadventure, *Into the Wild*, nor the movie by the same title, had yet come out, but all the locals knew the story of the young man who had perished in the wilderness after attempting to live on his own.

Sometimes I grew mad at McCandless for so needlessly throwing away his life in being ignorantly isolated in that bus — after all, a simple map, seeking the advice of locals, or even a basic field guide on edible plants could have prevented his death. At the same time, I completely understood his desire to be alone in the wilderness.

Our friends owned a bar in Healy called The Denali Smoke Shack. It was located near the entrance to Denali National Park and a crazy number of tourists funneled through their bar during the four-month summer season. I bartended there while Dee waitressed.

Pithecophilia

The Smoke Shack's speakers blasted Johnny Cash all day long, which suited the servers and cooks, most of whom thought of themselves as outlaws. A few times each month, a police officer would step into the smoky kitchen, cuff one of the cooks, and haul him away – usually for some prior offense in the lower forty-eight.

Dee and I had recently completed a one-year trip around the world. I thought I'd seen everything until I reached Alaska.

The scenery was breathtaking, majestic even, with the Alaska Range filling the horizon to the south. We camped in a forest of drunken pines; our tent set on a soft bed of taiga. The smells were intoxicating.

As the fall approached, the northern lights left me awestruck, feeling like anything was possible. And when I stood alone in the wilderness, I felt like someone was watching me.

Even the air felt charged with a primal electricity, which seemed to explain why the wolves howled or the elk bugled.

Aside from us humans, there were no apes within two thousand miles or more, but there were plenty of other animals to keep me occupied. Among them were black bears, wolves, caribou, deer, moose, lynx and wolverines.

There were also grizzlies. They visited our campsite at least once a day in search of food. The park boasted about four hundred of the bears. We were camped along the Nenana River, where they congregated en masse when the salmon were running.

I did entertain the thought of the bigfoot — or sasquatch — when I first arrived in Alaska. Who knows, maybe a *Gigantopithecus* from Asia crossed the Beringia land bridge like man. Perhaps they even co-existed in southeast Alaska with early humans for a while.

This might have inspired some of the legends.

There was no modern evidence of a great ape still living there; at least none that seemed plausible to me.

But, maybe, just maybe, there *was* a bigfoot lurking out there.

Of course, this may have just been my pithecophilia kicking in.

We had been on the road for a while and were happy to focus on work, and everything seemed to be going smoothly. Then, Dee got pregnant with our soon-to-be first-born daughter, Tavish.

I have often wondered if the fact that the baby was conceived on the Stampede Trail factored at all in her becoming a headstrong, fearless child. Maybe we should have chosen a tamer location.

Dee´s bouts of morning sickness soon turned into a problem: Even if I tossed the vomit a hundred yards away, the bears still followed the scent back to our site.

Suddenly we were woken nearly every morning by prowling grizzlies, sniffing and rubbing against the side of our wall tent.

By August, we had confirmed the pregnancy at a clinic in Fairbanks, and Dee decided to escape the coming cold—and the bears—and return to New England. August was still a summer month in Maine, where her mom lived, but things were already cooling down in Alaska.

I stayed an extra month to complete the season, working double shifts because the tourists wanted to stay up late to watch the northern lights.

One of the perks of being a bartender at the Denali Smoke Shack was the complimentary tours that I received for referring patrons to local outfitters. My last month in Alaska, I took three flights around Mt. Denali and got to white-water raft Denali Canyon a half dozen times.

It was like I was trying to stockpile my adrenaline for future use.

As soon as I was back in the lower forty-eight, with my wife, and the knowledge that I would soon be a father, I realized that I had to find a "real" job.

Within a few months we were living in Walpole, New Hampshire, and I was working for a travel office named Eos Study Tours. They created professionally-led educational tours for six nonprofit organizations. Three of the six organizations were scientific institutions: The Field Museum and Shedd Aquarium in Chicago, and the Denver Museum of Natural History.

For these groups, we tailored African safaris, archaeological tours, Mediterranean voyages, and river trips on the Amazon River. I worked in marketing, acting as a middleman between the organizations' lecturers, who led the groups, and the operators, who handled the logistics.

I had been traveling in Africa for years, living in my tent in game parks for about $350 a month. Now I was marketing ten-day safaris for $6,000 — plus airfare — in these same areas.

There was a part of me that ached to return to those places, to feel the adrenaline course through my veins as I scrambled my way into the Virunga Volcanoes. I consoled myself with the thought that this job was the closest I could get to adventure without leaving home.

What kept me rooted to my desk were the other three organizations: The Archaeological Institute of America, the American Geographical Society, and The Explorers Club.

The tours we created for these three groups were much more exciting: submersible dives to the *Titanic* and the *Bismarck*, Antarctic voyages on icebreakers, and private jet excursions to remote locations.

All of these outings were quite pricey and well beyond my personal financial reach, but I just loved the subject matter. For instance, there was a tour titled *The Search for the Source of the Nile*, which was a month-long private jet trip to important African sites where early explorers like Stanley, Livingstone, Burton, and Speke had been. Most of these places I'd visited myself.

The Search for the Source of the Nile journey, for instance, began with a stop in London to visit the Royal Geographic headquarters, where the curator opened the vault and let you handle Livingstone's actual journal.

"Dr. Livingstone, I presume..."

I had to stifle a laugh when I imagined some of our affluent customers traveling as I had in Zaire — nestled into the back of a truck, under a tarp, with a dozen or more Africans. Of course, this never happened – the organizations we supported spared no expense creating top-notch experiences with first-class transportation.

Another tour I liked was entitled *The Origins of Man in Southern Africa*, and it visited several significant hominin sites. The tour was led by Ian Tattersall, Ph.D., an expert in paleoanthropology and evolutionary theory.

The tour was a once-in-a-lifetime opportunity. I had visited many of these places but had few references other than my guidebook. I imagined how fulfilling it would be to see these sites and learn about their history and significance from a professional paleoanthropologist.

The best part of my job at Eos Study Tours was communicating with the operators and lecturers. I remember one day getting a marketing image from Robert Ballard's office that featured the *Bismarck* — a German battleship from World War II — sitting on the bottom of the Atlantic. There was a massive swastika still visible on the deck. Another day, Donald Johanson's office sent me some new images of Lucy — the most complete skeleton of an Australopithecine ever uncovered — for a brochure.

Some might consider this nerdy stuff, but these interactions fascinated me, and I ate it up.

Eos Study Tours was co-owned and directed by Todd Nielsen and his wife, Patricia Dooley. Nielsen had resurrected a bankrupt travel program, Discovery Tours, for the American Museum of Natural History, where he had worked for 17 years before forming his own company.

The Archaeological Institute of America (AIA) had some interesting excursions, exploring archaeological destinations like Egypt, Peru and Cambodia. Still, it was the tours we designed for The Explorers Club that really drew me in.

The Explorers Club was founded by a group of the world's leading explorers in 1904 and had about 3,000 members in 1999. This was an organization built on the accomplishments of individuals whom I'd worshipped in my youth, people like George Schaller, Dian Fossey, Carl Akeley and Theodore Roosevelt.

Everyone in the Explorers Club had a member I.D. that was always listed after their name. I couldn't help associating that with the themed names or numbers researchers assigned to apes in studies. But the brave men and women of The Explorers Club were far from comical. They were inspirational, and I found myself intimidated when I was in their presence. I was far from being the alpha male in this group.

A plaque on the wall boasted a few accomplishments of past members:

The Explorers Club
World Center for Exploration

First to the North Pole	1909
First to the South Pole	1911
First to the summit of Mount Everest	1953
First to the deepest point in the ocean	1960
First to the surface of the Moon	1969

I was told they left room at the bottom of the plaque for "First to the surface of Mars."

At one of my first visits to the club headquarters in New York City, I attended a meeting between my boss, Todd Nielsen, the president of the Club at the time, Captain Alfred McLaren, and Dr. Don Walsh.

We met in the Member's Lounge beneath a large painting of a herd of woolly rhinoceros.

Captain McLaren had helped map the floor of the Arctic Ocean, using a nuclear submarine, during the Cold War, and Dr. Walsh's accomplishment was just as ballsy. In 1960, Walsh and Jacques Piccard descended 35,810 feet to the bottom of the Mariana Trench in a special submarine called a bathyscaphe – they were the first to reach the deepest part of the ocean.

Both Walsh and McLaren lectured a fair amount for Eos Study Tours on deep-sea dives and arctic expeditions. While they discussed the details for the coming year's excursions with my boss, I drifted about the lobby.

In one anteroom, there was a large globe. Legend had it that Thor Heyerdahl had first proposed his *Kon-Tiki* voyage while huddled around that globe. The scene was reenacted in the movie *Kon-Tiki*.

Their objective was to show that people from South America were the first to settle Polynesia. With a five-person crew, Heyerdahl mostly drifted on a balsa-wood raft 4,300 miles from Peru to Polynesia to show that this was possible.

I continued up the long winding staircase, deeper into the incredible building. It was designed as an urban version of an English manor house - all brick, marble, mahogany and leaded glass. Everywhere I looked, the building had been embellished with loving, stately detail, from the wood paneling around the fireplaces to the plaster birds set into the ceiling.

I ascended past a suspended Arctic supply sledge and a monstrous stuffed polar bear. The second floor housed the archives, which includes the Expedition Flags. Today, there are 202 of them, and each has its own unique history. A flag was carried on all of the Apollo missions.

The accomplishments of these explorers were dizzying.

I stopped to examine Flag number 2, which accompanied Roy Chapman Andrews into the Gobi Desert in 1925. Andrews, the real-life inspiration for Indiana Jones.

The staircase continued up, past photos and displays that lined the walls: Club presidents, medalists and explorers; searchers who could not rest until they pushed the boundaries of exploration and scientific knowledge. Their names echo throughout history, and I heard them whisper to me as I stared at their photos: Peary, Amundsen, Shackleton and Roosevelt. Sir Edmund Hillary and Tenzing Norgay. And names from the Space Age, too, like Yeager, Glenn, Armstrong, and Aldrin.

There were many notable women explorers as well. Astronaut Sally Ride, oceanographer Dr. Sylvia Earle, and primatologist Dr. Jane Goodall, to name just a few.

By the time I reached the fifth-floor landing and glanced into the gallery with its enormous, vaulted ceiling, I felt about as significant as a speck of sand in the desert.

I had traveled to about a hundred countries and crossed many of them overland, but that seemed insignificant compared to these accomplishments. At the end of the hall, above the fireplace and flanked by two enormous elephant tusks, hung a portrait of Arctic explorer Peter Freuchen.

I didn't know who he was at the time but felt certain he'd accomplished much more exploration than I ever would. Still, something about being there, in that hall, made me feel I was connected to these great men and women.

By seeing their faces and examining the strange relics from all over the world, I felt like I was sharing these adventures. I meandered through the expansive room and let my gaze float through the plethora of items: a woolly mammoth tusk, a totem pole from New Guinea, a rare book chronicling Napoleon's 1798 expedition to Egypt, and a narwhal tusk.

There's even the penis of a sperm whale, which gave me pause. As I chuckled to myself, I realized there was someone in the hall with me.

Next to the fireplace, an older gentleman was staring at a stuffed cheetah. I commented that I had seen one catch an impala on the Serengeti, and he, in turn, shared a story of witnessing two cheetahs in Kenya's Masai Mara game reserve.

He introduced himself as Neil, and forty-five minutes of swapping stories about African adventures ensued. I told him of my obsession with apes, which led to another round of trading stories. This man had been to many places on the African continent, but I had seen my share too, and I felt proud that I could boast about my exploits on almost equal footing.

Here was someone that might be welcome in my tribe, a kindred spirit whose accomplishments didn't wholly overshadow mine.

Neil said he thought I had lived an exciting life. I soaked up the praise, and I would have talked to him all day if a staffer hadn't stuck his head in the door and summoned him with a hand gesture.

Ten minutes later, I discovered that the nice older man I'd been talking with—who was, in fact, quite an accomplished explorer—had gone way beyond Africa in his travels, including being the first human to set foot on the moon.

So much for equal footing.

But that's The Explorers Club—one is constantly surrounded by giants.

Our travel office employed a woman named Penelope Bodry-Sanders, who helped coordinate lecturers for various Eos tours. She was a long-time member of the Explorers Club and had served in the Library and Archives Committee. Prior to working with my company, she worked for the American Museum of Natural History (AMNH) in the Library and then for AMNH Discovery Tours for eighteen years.

It was at AMNH that she was exposed to the incredible African dioramas created by Carl Akeley, something I had yet to see and always wanted to.

Akeley's Hall of African Mammals brought these animals to the public's attention in an unprecedented way. In most cases, this would be the only way the public would ever see these animals. Thus, it created a platform for education.

When Akeley first studied the mountain gorillas in 1921, he felt that few remained, and he warned that unless the Virungas were protected, they would go extinct in a few years. Many believe that without his efforts, there would be no mountain gorillas today.

The beginning of the 19th century was the age of the great white hunter. It was hunters turned conservationists like Carl Akeley and Theodore Roosevelt—who shot many of the animals displayed in the Hall—that took the first steps to set aside land to save the animals.

Penelope Bodry-Sanders eventually published a book: *African Obsession: The Life and Legacy of Carl Akeley*. Akeley had died mysteriously in Africa, and in 1990 Bodry-Sanders made a trek to the location of his death, high in the Virungas, where she rediscovered and redecorated his gravesite.

And where was it? On the slopes of Mt. Mikeno, in an alpine meadow called Kabara. The same place I had peered at through the misty morning fog. The same place Carl Akeley first encountered the apes, followed by George Schaller, and then Dian Fossey.

It was the place that I still dreamed about when my mind wandered. I may have fooled my employer that I was ready to settle for an office job, but my pithecophilia never faded.

Hidden inside me, I knew there were things I had left undone, and truths I had yet to uncover.

A voice deep within me whispered, "Come on, Kiboko, the jungle awaits you."

The Explorers Club gallery. Top floor. 1999.

Mantled Howler Monkey (*Alouatta palliata*).
Habitat: Tropical dry forest & rain forests. Range: Central & South America.

Chapter Fifteen

The Sahelanthropus
(2000)

Near the end of my first year with Eos Study Tours I qualified for a fam—or complimentary—tour. I would go on one of the excursions that we marketed as an "inspection."

My friend, Penelope Bodry-Sanders, had encouraged me to join The Explorers Club and sponsored me to get in, and now I was a proud member. Suddenly it didn't seem so bad to have a desk job.

I desperately wanted to get to Antarctica—the one continent I had yet to see—but there were no openings on any of our current trips.

In fact, the only excursion we marketed with room for me was an observation platform in the middle of the Panamanian jungle. Given my past history with Panama, I wasn't really itching to return. Memories of enraged people—yellow-eyed from hepatitis—chasing me through the streets still haunted me from time to time.

So, there's a bad side to having that default brain network. If I lived in the moment, like most of the creatures in the animal kingdom, my mind would not endlessly return to traumatic events or worry about what dangers may await in Panama.

191

It would leave me alone.

But the contemplative side of my brain would not let it go. Aarg, the curse of sapience: remembering. My restless mind flashed image after image of angry people staring at me coldly. And that is a hard one to shake because anger is a burning in the mind: It consumes people. When anger is present, it vanquishes compassion like the noonday sun kills a shadow.

All these thoughts racing through my mind caused me to vacillate for a while. But I ultimately decided to travel to Panama.

I had a one-year-old child now, a steady job, and opportunities to travel did not come up often. I consoled myself with a promise to get out of Panama City quickly and get into the rainforest.

And my destination, Canopy Tower, seemed like the perfect place to experience that hot, sticky jungle and forget about humankind. The Tower sat on a hillside within Soberanía National Park. It featured an observation platform, set fifty feet above the ground, and offered a 360-degree view of the treetops and the surrounding jungle. As you can imagine, it was a birder's paradise.

Unfortunately, when I arrived at Tocumen airport, my mind was immediately overrun with turbulent memories. As I entered the lavatory, I suddenly and vividly remembered getting sick in that same bathroom twelve years ago. I could almost see my younger self, cleaning up frantically so I could board the flight and pretending to be healthy.

I recalled how much I worried that the attendants would discover I was sick—with hepatitis, I eventually learned—and bring me to the hospital instead of letting me fly. Locals had warned me that the country was about to descend into chaos because their de-facto president at the time, Manuel Noriega, had grown unstable. As an American, there was no place that I'd be safe, not even in a hospital bed.

I realize now it was irresponsible for me to travel when I was possibly contagious. But at the time, I feared for my life.

I shook off the memories. When I emerged from the airport, a man waited with my name on a sign. I was then driven through the central part of the city.

My heart raced. My vision began to tunnel, and I felt I might black out.

It had been over a decade, but I still felt compelled to scan the crowds for my lost friend Vendu. I was paranoid, and my mind jumped from face to face, pausing on the ones I suddenly didn't trust.

At my desk in New Hampshire, I had yearned for adventure, but now that I was traveling again, it seemed fear was all I felt.

Luckily, my driver had no intention of lingering, and soon we were out of the city, speeding along mile after mile of jungle-lined highway. I knew from scanning maps that only a short distance from Panama City were two national parks: Soberanía National Park, at 56,000 acres, and the much larger Chagres National Park with 318,000 acres.

These parks contain an incredible diversity of species, preserved in part due to the Panama Canal. Among the most impressive animals occurring there is the endangered Harpy Eagle, which has a 7-foot wingspan, and the Bushmaster, the world's largest viper. If a major highway had been constructed along this corridor, most of the area would have been developed.

The Tower was formally a twelve-sided radar installation run by the U.S. Army. After it was decommissioned, it became a tourist destination. Of the three floors, the first two were converted into a dozen guest rooms. They were comfortably furnished with hammocks, mosquito nets, cozy beds, and had large windows.

The top floor contained the dining area, with couches, more hammocks, and a well-stocked library with teak shelves.

My driver said goodbye after carrying my bag to the reception, and soon I was in my room. I collapsed on the bed and tried to shake off the panic that had gripped me since the airport.

Before the sun began to lighten the sky the next morning, everyone was gathered on the roof to see what birds would show up.

Panama's unique location on the isthmus between North and South America is responsible for the large number of species that exist there because there are both resident and migratory animals. Over 1,500 bird and animal species occur in Panama; more than 250 bird species have been cataloged from the tower alone.

On an average morning, the guests could observe many species, including parrots, toucans, blue cotingas, short-tailed hawks and much more.

I got up with everyone else and checked off what birds I saw in a field notebook the staff had given me, but I had yet to develop an appreciation for birding at that point in my life.

I stayed in a hammock on the observation platform all morning, trying to relax and not think about Panama in 1988.

Eventually, I got up for lunch, but later, I returned to my hammock in the lazier hours of the sweltering afternoon. I tried to channel the black and white colobus monkeys I had seen at Elsamere, and just chill.

I watched a two-toed sloth slowly move up a tree.

I observed a beautiful blue butterfly flutter by.

I swayed with the gentle breeze.

Then I closed my eyes and listened to the chorus of birdcalls.

But I was still restless, and the distant, rolling thunder seemed to whisper that I should be moving.

Later that day, I was approached by the proprietor, a man named Raul. Sitting eye-level with the treetops, the jungle was alive with creaks, rustling leaves, and other sounds that should have intrigued me, but I had been staring off in the distance, lost in thought.

"You do not care much for the birds," stated Raul.

I shook my head, politely, "Don't worry about me. This place is great. I'm not sure why I'm so fidgety."

He nodded. "Perhaps you would like to take a hike. Have you ever heard of the Cruces Trail?"

I told him I had not, and he said he would arrange everything for the next day.

After the Conquistadors absconded the riches from the Inca, who resided from modern-day Peru to Chile in the 16th century, they needed to transport it to Spain. They could have gone south and tried their luck on Cape Horn but instead opted to forge the Cruces Trail and cross the Isthmus of Panama.

At its narrowest point, the county is about fifty miles wide, and rivers can be used to navigate a large section of that. What remained was a fifteen-mile stretch of land through dense rainforest. So, the Conquistadors blazed a trail right through it. In some sections, they improved the trail with dry-laid stone to help prevent it from washing out. Even after 400 years, these cobblestones are still visible.

This trail was tremendously important to the Spanish. At one point, they were moving over 2,000 tons of silver and gold a year in caravans of up to 1,000 mules. Once they reached the end of the trail, they were met by ships on the Chagres River. From there, the plunder could be ferried downstream to the Caribbean Sea and eventually across the Atlantic Ocean to Spain.

Despite its diminutive distance, this short crossing claimed many lives. Renegade slaves from Haiti — maroons — hid along the trail and attacked the caravans when they passed.

Malaria and other mosquito-borne diseases killed them in droves. Spiky poisonous trees and deadly snakes are common here. Few knew how to survive in the jungle, and if a man got lost or separated during an attack, he was rarely seen again.

I set out with a guide the next day after breakfast. From the tower, it was a short walk to connect with the Cruces Trail. We spoke Spanish, and my limited command of that language kept our exchanges to a minimum. Luckily, I had read up on the area.

Although this section of Central America is almost 3.5 million years old, it represents some of the geologically youngest land on Earth. Yet to me, it felt ancient and prehistoric.

Pre-Columbian Peoples may have cleared much of the jungle earlier on, but the rainforest now seemed untouched. Ancient vines and immense trees soared up into a canopy, ninety feet above, and the emergent layer rose to one hundred and thirty feet in some areas.

Because the jungle is so dense, wildlife is rarely seen. But it was exciting to know the jungle is full of tapirs, ocelots, prehensile-tailed porcupines, anteaters, armadillos, white-faced capuchins, tamarins and capybaras with manatees, crocodiles, and caimans inhabiting the surrounding waters.

About halfway through our hike it started to rain — hard. I had a waterproof outer shell in my daypack, and I put it on. Although I was protected from the rain now, I was already soaking wet. With the humidity of the jungle, I began to sweat like I was in a sauna.

For the next few hours, the rain fell upon us with a vengeance, relentlessly and driving. It seemed unwilling to ease up, and soon the jungle floor became saturated. From time to time, we trudged through shin-deep water.

We stopped for lunch under the shelter of a toppled Guanacaste tree, whose trunk was six feet wide. The lush, moss-covered ground lay soaked. Clouds of mist were rising from the puddles. Water cascaded down the tree trunks, rain constantly fell from above, and the entire jungle shivered water whenever a gust blew through.

My guide made a gesture that I didn't understand and disappeared into the jungle, leaving me alone.

There were no sounds other than the falling rain.

Dark clouds overhead shed a gloomy light on the rainforest, and I got the spooks. Under my raincoat I could feel the hair on my forearms stand up.

I looked around. I don't think I've ever felt so alone.

There are no apes in Panama, only monkeys, but for some reason I began to imagine that an ape-like creature was in this wet forest.

Watching me.

Being alone in the wilderness can do strange things to one's mind.

I thought of the early hominin from *Altered States*—the one that crawled out of the isolation tank.

And beyond all logic, I felt it was close.

In my head, it was a *Sahelanthropus*, one of our earliest ancestors, dating back more than 6 million years. While I knew these hominins were known only from Africa, I could still see it clearly. It was not quite four feet tall, bipedal, flattened skull with a low brow. Arms elongate, legs short and stubby, and its entire body was covered in fur.

I imagined this hominin traveling through the wet terrain. Small, but fierce-looking. Graceful, with a recognizable human form. Cautiously scanning both the ground and the canopy above.

And ravenously hungry, with yellow teeth that were even and very human in appearance.

In my mind, the apelike creature looked in my direction, curled its lips and bared its teeth.

I shuddered.

I steeled my nerves and scanned the jungle around me.

A bush shook violently about twenty feet away. Under the din of the rain, I couldn't hear anything. My eyes bulged as I stared at it.

I almost had a heart attack when my guide stepped out from the brush, ready to set out again. Man, was I jumpy.

We had been hiking for hours, although I had no sense of direction because I couldn't see the sun. But I figured we must be close to the Chagres River when the water rose above our knees. It didn't seem normal for a jungle to flood this much, even with the intense rain.

Indeed, my guide explained that the river had overrun its banks.

We could not see a river, only the immediate, dripping jungle directly around us. Through breaks in the canopy, I glimpsed black-bellied clouds lingering above, eclipsing the sun. It felt like we were in some dim underworld.

The going was slow on the flooded trail, and the guide began to worry about making our connection with a boat that was to be waiting on the watercourse. He decided to scout ahead and instructed me nervously to stay where I was until he returned.

He said the words in English as if to stress their importance. He wanted no misunderstandings. "Please wait here. No move. Please."

I nodded that I understood, and that I would remain rooted exactly where I was.

With that, he left me, standing in knee-deep water while the rain continued to pelt the jungle. It didn't take long for me to feel completely alone, again. As I scanned the green world around me, I remembered that this was also the world of jaguars and pumas.

Forget about my imaginary hominin; this jungle bore real threats.

There were also plenty of snakes, and I wondered what I would do if a bushmaster, or perhaps a fer-de-lance — a venomous snake that can grow to eight feet — suddenly appeared slithering toward me.

Then, I heard howlers.

Mantled Howler Monkeys (*Alouatta palliata*) are found throughout this jungle, and apparently, a troop was in the trees above me. They are the largest of the new world monkeys, just under three feet tall with a long, prehensile tail.

They have the loudest call of any primate, and they roar at sunrise and sunset to delineate their territory. Their calls can travel for miles through the dense rainforest.

But what I like best about the howlers is that they sometimes howl right before a storm arrives.

And they don't do it from the safe shelter under a tree. Nope, they climb to the top and howl at the approaching storm.

As if they are trying to scare it off.

Or maybe they are exclaiming a defiant, "Bring it!"

Whenever a rumble of thunder shook the jungle, a few of them barked back in response, and I scanned the canopy with trepidation.

I couldn't tell how many there were up there, but it sounded like at least a dozen. I stared at my feet, planted in the swirling dark water, and hoped they would stay in the tree. I was out of my element here, and maybe I feared things unnecessarily, but a voice in my mind stupidly keep saying I should run — not that I'd even know where to run to.

In fact, even to stumble thirty feet from my location might lead to me being hopelessly lost; the water completely obscured the cobblestone trail.

Then, the booming thunder and the crack of lightning crept closer. I realized a big storm was moving in. The howlers sensed it too and were growing more agitated overhead. With the first low rumble, they screamed in response. The louder the thunder, the louder they bellowed until it seemed one and the same.

I thought of the *Sahelanthropus* I had dreamed up and could imagine him doing the same thing. At that moment, nothing seemed more natural than shouting at an approaching storm.

Bring it! I thought.

The next thing I knew, I was standing in the most intense downpour I had ever experienced. The water crashed and spiraled down from above. It felt like buckets of water were being poured directly on me.

And then it mysteriously let up - just as a bolt of lightning hit so close that the thunder was instantaneous. I was thunderstruck.

But the deafening boom did not deter the howlers.

Their calls seemed even louder now that the storm was upon us.

I threw back my hood and listened. It was the most powerful, primal thing I had ever experienced. It seemed like their howls opened a door in my heart from which I could release any pent-up frustrations.

It made my own worries and cares feel inconsequential and melt away.

It made me feel like the only thing that deserved my attention now was the storm above us.

I shrugged off the fear that I had carried since my arrival.

Pithecophilia

The thing I called "me" had simply dissolved in the rain, and in its place, something else appeared. Something ape-like that also wanted to howl.

Listening to their roar, I felt connected to the howlers, and the other apes and monkeys I'd spent time with over the years: The orangutans in Sumatra, Papillion on the Thai islands, Oscar in the Virungas — even Shirley, the baboon. I felt their eyes on me.

I remembered the stare of the mountain gorilla in my old photo.

And when the howlers next roared, I felt whatever I'd sensed was common within us rising to the surface.

I wished I was above the trees, in the canopy, with them.

I raised my face to the sky and roared at the heavens.

It was a cry that came from my soul, and I felt my eyes flood with tears as it rose from my throat. As if this howl had been captive for years and was only now escaping.

I felt free, unrestrained. I felt alive. And I howled until I was hoarse, and the storm had passed.

When the guide returned ten minutes later, I was exhausted. I didn't mention the howlers, who had become quiet once the storm had passed.

I followed him through the jungle silently. At this point, the water had risen past my hips. I then spied the boat, waiting.

By the time I climbed aboard, the storm was long gone. The insect and bird calls filled the air once again. It seemed magical, and I felt enchanted as I took it in quietly.

On the ride back, the sun broke through the clouds, and that sweltering heat reclaimed the land.

Within a few days I was home again.

But to this day, when I witness a fierce storm, I can hear the howlers bellowing behind the din of rain.

The cobblestoned Cruces Trail.
Soberania Nat. Park, Panama. 2000.

Carl Akeley's gorilla diorama, Hall of African Mammals.
New York City, NY. 2010.

The cobblestoned Cruces Trail.
Soberania Nat. Park, Panama. 2000.

Carl Akeley's gorilla diorama, Hall of African Mammals.
New York City, NY. 2010.

Chapter Sixteen

AMNH
(2010)

I dreamt of adventure often when I was a kid. It began with tales my mother told me — wild yarns about exotic animals and forgotten tribes. When my father purchased some land in northern Maine, my adventurous cerebral wanderings would soon also include our 26th president, Theodore Roosevelt.

Our land in Aroostook County was purchased from a man named William Sewall, whose grandfather — also named William Sewall — had been Roosevelt's guide when he first explored the Maine wilderness in his youth.

Roosevelt had arrived in Island Falls, Maine, in 1878 when he was a sickly young man of twenty. His father, Theodore Roosevelt, Sr., known to the people of New York City as Greatheart, had died the year before, and the young man was still clearly suffering from the loss.

Yet the Maine woods and the guidance of Sewall seemed to work miraculously on him. Within a year, he was physically robust, training daily in shooting, boxing, and running. Some of this metamorphosis may have been due to meeting the love of his life, his first wife, Alice Hathaway Lee, whom he courted during this time.

He visited Maine three times during the coming twelve months, and as far as I could see, this was the year he became a man.

I developed a friendship with William Sewell's wife, Cleo. In my twenties, she entertained me with stories about young Roosevelt's time in northern Maine and how this experience turned him into an outdoorsman.

I would visit Cleo upon returning from my travels. While I regaled her with my own tales, she would let me hold a pocket watch that "TR" had given her husband's grandfather. Later, Cleo's son David would show me the rifle, pistol and saddle Roosevelt had used when he was a Badlands rancher.

TR's father, Theodore Roosevelt, Sr., was a philanthropist and helped found some of New York's greatest institutions, including the New York City Children's Aid Society, the Metropolitan Museum of Art, and the American Museum of Natural History.

In 1869, Roosevelt, Sr. drafted the charter to establish the American Museum of Natural History in the parlor of his home. His ten-year-old son Teddy was there and officially donated twelve animal specimens that he had carefully preserved. Thus began the first collection for what would become the largest natural history museum in the world. Today the museum is comprised of 45 permanent exhibition halls, a planetarium, and a library.

And I can imagine how excited young Roosevelt had been about the creation of the museum. This was the golden age of exploration, which lasted from 1880 to 1930. Soon, AMNH scientists were traipsing through remote landscapes on every continent, from the Poles to the jungles to the equatorial deserts. The specimens and artifacts they brought back began to fill the display cases.

Sunday newspapers were teeming with articles, written like field dispatches, of museum men encountering exotic tribes and dangerous animals.

I followed along — a hundred years later — and still felt the thrill of uncovering unknown places and facts. My dreams were overflowing with prehistoric creatures, rare animals, pygmies, giants and cannibals.

And, of course, apes. After all, these explorers were the very guys who hoped to come across the last *Gigantopithecus*, a yeti, or a relict dinosaur still living in Patagonia. At the peak of this nationwide craze, AMNH supported as many as forty expeditions a year.

In 1909, following his second term as President of the United States, Roosevelt went on a hunting expedition to Africa with his son Kermit to collect specimens for the Smithsonian and AMNH. Many of these preserved animals are still on display at the Mammals Hall in the Smithsonian Museum of Natural History.

It was on this expedition that he got to know Carl Akeley, and an elephant that Roosevelt shot ended up in AMNH's Hall of African Mammals.

The American public eagerly ingested the widespread publicity that followed Roosevelt's African safari, and soon others followed. And thus began the era of the great white hunter.

In 1921, Carl Akeley traveled to Africa to obtain specimens for the Great African Hall at AMNH, among them mountain gorillas. During this expedition, a change came over the man, and like Roosevelt, he was transformed from a hunter to a conservationist.

But not before he had collected his specimens.

The newspapers followed his exploits, one speculating that he had brought women along to attract male gorillas out of the jungle.

But what Akeley wanted to do was something the world had never seen. His dream was to represent the boundless mysteries of the mighty African continent in forty dioramas—to offer people a three-dimensional glimpse of what he had experienced.

He created his dioramas with the help of professional artists, capturing the spirit of the locations by having the artists paint realistic backdrops and then filling the display with replicas of African plants and shrubs. This was before color photography became popular. So, the public had never seen anything like this.

Akeley also rejected traditional mounting, preferring to show the animals feeding, playing, or fighting. And to make sure this would be as realistic as possible, he took the artists into the field with him.

Today, the American Museum of Natural History is visited by about five million people a year. It boasts a collection of over 33 million specimens of plants, animals, fossils, rocks, minerals, and meteorites, as well as human remains and cultural artifacts.

The museum still sponsors over 120 field expeditions a year.

These explorations ferried me through my youth, only being overtaken by the Apollo missions, and finally, Neil Armstrong setting foot on the moon.

But as cool as it seemed to fly through space, as a boy, I still desperately wanted to stand next to an ape in the wild.

In 1926, Akeley returned to Africa. His Hall of African Mammals project was proceeding smoothly, and work would continue while he was securing more specimens in Africa. He had mostly completed the gorilla diorama but still needed the backdrop, and a small herd of charging elephants had been assembled in place in the center of the Hall.

He wanted to locate the exact spot where he had shot a male gorilla five years before. The body of that gorilla was now on display at AMNH, along with several other family members. Akeley had named the gorilla the Lone Male of Karisimbi, and he was determined to have the diorama background correctly illustrate the actual panorama.

On the expedition was the American painter, William Robinson Leigh, whose task was to capture the scene.

Akeley appeared sickly, pale and weak, as he ascended the slopes of Mt. Mikeno. But he was thrilled to be back in the Virungas. When his expedition members first arrived, they encountered a group of gorillas feasting on wild celery, and he thought it a good sign.

On May 19th, he celebrated his 62nd birthday.

He was frail but pressed on into the mountains, leading the artist painting the diorama, Leigh, to the very spot where the Lone Male was shot.

But on his return to camp, he succumbed to whatever illness had plagued him and shortly after died.

We can only speculate on what killed him. Was it malaria, typhoid, or dysentery? Or it may have been acute mountain sickness or even simple exhaustion.

Akeley was buried near where he died – in a peaceful meadow in the saddle between Mt. Mikeno and Mt. Karisimbi.

Akeley's Hall finally opened in 1936, on what would have been his 72nd birthday. When completed, there were only 28 dioramas — instead of the proposed 40. But otherwise, it was almost exactly as he imagined it. The Hall offers compelling glimpses into Africa, pulling the spectator away from their world and into another.

I still yearned to see it, but I had moved to the Southwest a decade earlier and had not found an excuse to go to New York City. I also had a house full of growing daughters to wrangle and not a lot of free time.

But I had the Hall in my sights. It was on my bucket list.

You may ask why I would want to see a bunch of dead animals. And I suppose it's a pertinent question. And why venerate Akeley, who had actually killed gorillas?

Was the creation of his spectacular Hall justification?

In the case of the Lone Male of Karisimbi, maybe.

After Akeley returned from Africa in 1921, he wasted no time convincing King Albert of Belgium to create a national park to protect mountain gorillas and their habitat. By 1929 — just when the age of the white hunter was ramping up — 190 square miles of the Virunga volcano chain was set aside and established as the Albert National Park.

In doing this, back then, Akeley was credited with having saved the mountain gorillas from extinction.

And he bore the thought of the national park in his heart when he made that last visit. Maybe it gave him a little solace regarding the killing he'd done.

Perhaps he knew he was dying and wanted to be in the Virungas when he did.

Pithecophilia

The killing of the gorillas had weighed heavily on him. He had a growing sense of being "the savage, the aggressor, the murderer."

His conundrum was this: The only way to prevent people from hunting mountain gorillas to extinction is to shoot a few and use them to educate the public on the necessity of preserving their habitat.

At least that's how he saw it—but following through proved difficult. In the process of tracking and observing the mountain gorillas, his attitude changed.

He noted that when the gorillas experienced pain or terror, he could see it in their eyes in a familiar way. He saw them as intelligent and sensitive.

And maybe that's why killing gorillas for his exhibit was the beginning of the end of Akeley. Today he's known as Africa's biographer and poet. To me, it seems that getting to know Africa, and its animals, on such an intimate level came with a cost.

The gorilla diorama was completed with the backdrop Akeley wanted, making it an even more personal monument to the man, as it now depicted the site of the death of the Lone Male of Karisimbi – as well as his own.

In the fall of 2010, I finally made it to the American Museum of Natural History. While visiting my parents in New Hampshire, I decided to drive down to New York City.

I made the four-hour journey with a whole bunch of family, including my parents, Patricia and Ron, my sister Kathy, and her three boys, Dean, Greg, and baby Sammy.

My own clan had continued to expand. My oldest, Tavish—the one conceived on the Stampede Trail—was now eleven, and her younger sister, Saydrin, had just turned nine.

And Dee had the bulge of another child under her fall coat, who would be born on January 11, 2011. 1-11-11.

Our third daughter, Martika.

We entered through the Theodore Roosevelt Rotunda.

In front of us, the skeleton of a long-necked dinosaur reared up from another attacking dinosaur.

"The tall one is a barosaurus," said Dean, my oldest nephew.

Dean had all the markings of a future scientist, and I was proud to bring him here. At seven, he knew more birds, dinosaurs, and constellations than I ever would.

"The other one is an allosaurus," he added, and would have said more had not his younger brothers grabbed him and start shaking him while yelling, "Raawwwww!!"

A dinosaur attack led by a ten-month-old.

The rotunda was created as a memorial to Theodore Roosevelt. Three massive murals depicted different events from the president's life.

In one, Roosevelt received the Nobel Peace Prize, and I remembered that he was the first American to receive this honor. In another section, he was hunting and collecting specimens in Africa.

I stepped closer to the third mural and could make out TR at the Panama Canal. For a brief instant, I heard the howler monkeys calling me.

The powerful recollection shook me for a moment, and then I came back to my senses, and I looked around for the rest of my group.

We were supposed to gather before heading into the museum.

I looked across the room and saw Dee returning with the tickets but spotted no one else. Even my girls were absent—no doubt led off by Tavish, who always seemed hellbent on finding her own way.

Ten minutes later, I had them all. My parents had been in the lavatory, my sister and her boys had drifted towards the Butterfly Conservatory, while my daughters were in the gift shop.

We stood in a group by the towering dinosaur while Dee passed out the tickets. This was my big moment, and I wanted to steer everyone into the Akeley Hall of African Mammals before we went our separate ways.

But in the few seconds it took me to read one of the Roosevelt quotes on the wall, it seemed every one of them set off in different directions.

"Stop!" I yelled, a little too loud.

They all stopped—including a few tourists near us—and when I pointed at the African Hall and added, "In there!" they moved in unison that way.

We entered the Hall, and right away, my girls ran deeper into the room, past the charging elephants in the center. My parents took a seat to take it all in, while Dee and my sister walked along with the boys, holding the toddler's hand.

I took a few steps to the left and stopped dead in my tracks.

My nephew Dean shook my arm and asked if I would take him to see the Scales of the Universe, but I hardly heard him.

Before me was Akeley's gorilla diorama, and it took my breath away.

I had wanted to see this display for most of my life. I'd read about Akeley and his trek to Africa. I had stood where he had been inspired to build this diorama.

Yet I had never seen it. And now that I finally did, I experienced a revelation that seemed to encompass my entire life. This rattled me so much that I felt I couldn't look at the diorama directly.

My eyes avoided the large gorilla standing in the middle of it.

Instead, I examined the backdrop, painted from the location where both the Lone Male of Karisimbi and Carl Akeley had died. I recalled staring at the same vista from Mt. Sabyinyo.

In the distance were two towering volcanos, Mount Nyiragongo and Mount Nyamuragira. I remembered peering at them through yellow sunlight, and my guide telling me they were about twenty-five miles away.

Smoke was rising from their cones, and a few clouds clung to their flanks as they slanted downward toward the saddle. I felt like I was there, the humidity seeping into my clothes, the smell of earth heavy in the air.

The diorama was framed by trees — moss-covered hagenia with thick vines trailing down. Dense brush covered the ground.

It seemed if I closed my eyes, I would hear birds singing.

I let my eyes trail over several other gorillas in the display.

A female. Several adolescents.

I lingered on them, stalling...

Finally, I let my eyes settle on the Lone Male.

My hunch had been correct the moment I saw the diorama. And now, after examining it up close, I knew.

The photo my teacher had made for me all those years ago — the one that had set me out on my journey of encountering an ape in the wild — had been of this diorama, not of a living ape.

I remembered the nights throughout my youth when I would wake and stare at that image.

And I felt a pang of sorrow at the thought that this gorilla had been dead nearly eighty years. While I had been in the Virungas, I'd wondered if he could still be alive, but I knew now that by the time I went there, even his grandchildren had most likely been long gone.

Akeley's face passed before my eyes, and I felt anger at the man who had killed this gorilla.

Yet, while I peered at the ape, I reflected on how Akeley had used this display to educate the public and how his efforts had ultimately saved the mountain gorillas.

I had been able to see them in real life because of his contributions. And a photo of his diorama inspired me to roam the earth in search of apes. To commune with them.

I realized this mountain gorilla had no say in this. He'd been murdered after all, but still, his image had changed me. And during my travels, I'd felt he had been with me.

I thought of the Roosevelt quote I had read in the rotunda, "Keep your eyes on the stars and keep your feet on the ground."

So, I let the sadness fade away, and instead, let the ape encounters I had experienced fill my heart. Because apes had helped me through the most difficult times of my life, times when had I not been filled with wonder, I may have been overcome with grief or fear.

When I was lost in Sumatra, being found by those orangutans gave me hope and helped me retain my sanity. Even after it grew dark and I clung to a tree in fear, there was a part of me that felt I had friends in the jungle.

When I was injured in Thailand, I felt a kinship in "doing time" with Papillon.

And I had been drawn to the howlers in Panama because my heart was still troubled by the mob that had attacked me twelve years earlier. Maybe I had needed to release this trauma, and I had found no way to do that in this so-called modern world.

I have so many memories of primates. I sensed their eyes on me — sneaky vervets and capuchins, playful gibbons, laidback colobus monkeys and sharp-eyed langurs, curious orangutans and majestic gorillas. And so many more: howlers, baboons, macaques and squirrel monkeys... they all watched me with a simian knowing that I was finally coming to understand.

The gorilla in front of me was responsible for those experiences.

I hoped somehow the Lone Male could know how important he had been to me.

I had gone through life feeling like we had a connection.

His image had served as a focal point for my dreams.

I smiled at him now and wished he could somehow know how very much I had loved him all these years.

Somehow his story had become mine, and I hoped mine, his.

"Hi," I said, and then added with a grin, "it's me, Kiboko."

I stood there for some time, staring into his eyes, while the great African Hall spun around us. I wanted to say so much to this gorilla, but in the end, I only nodded, wiped away a tear, and said, "Thank you."

The Lone Male of Karisimbi. AMNH. 2010.

My mountain gorilla photo. 1976.

Pithecophilia

Final Thoughts

2020

Pithecophilia

Author's note

Hominization
(2020)

Around two years of age, most young children pass the same milestones. They take their first few steps, make their first social smile, and utter their first words. Soon after, they manifest examples of self-awareness through emotions like embarrassment and pride.

Before the age of two, they are conscious but not self-aware.

Yet, in those early months, their minds are still highly active.

The growing awareness inside them is limited by a lack of language and experience but can still be found, implicitly, in the perceptions and actions of the infant.

But when one observes a toddler, one does not sense that they are limited in some way.

It is the opposite. They seem to innately possess the ability to learn.

Indeed, it could be argued that this is what they do best.

They explore and learn — spurred by their insatiable curiosity.

My wife and I raised three daughters. And I will never forget staring into their innocent infant eyes, wondering what they were thinking. I spent a lot of time doing this, hoping to get a clue about the persona that was soon to emerge.

Yet, that young infant mind remained a mystery to me.

When they stared back at me, all I could see was wonder.

I read about humans that function without an "inner dialogue" and couldn't imagine what that would be like. People who heard no voice in their minds when they thought.

Merely thinking about thinking puts you squarely in the part of the brain called the "default mode network." When you think of your past or future, or your opinions, this is where you reside. It is the seat of the running narrative in your head.

How could a mind work without that narrative?

I found my confusion compounded when I started to contemplate the minds of various animals. Some, like the great apes, show clear signs of being self-aware; whereas so many others appear to possess consciousness but do not seem to be self-aware. I simply could not wrap my head around how the latter might perceive their world.

The problem I discovered when writing this collection of stories was that I feared I was limiting primates with the thoughts that I had given them, that I might be condensing them into cute, cozy creatures with simple minds. As I pointed out, our species developed a default mode network after we split from the common primate ancestor – what could I suggest was there in its place?

In humans, inner dialogue is produced by generating language and not articulating, so how would that work with apes? As we know, other apes do not use words. Could a series of images create the same effect? I can only imagine that is what is happening when my dog is dreaming.

The default mode is also the center of depression and anxiety, so perhaps they are better off than us in that regard.

My dilemma is that I put a lot of stock on the importance of that part of my brain, but I utterly fail to understand what occurs in the consciousness of other living creatures.

If I can't grasp what happens in the mind of my one-year-old child, how can I conceptualize the complex songs humpback whales exchange through the deep ocean waters or interpret the changing colors and body language between two octopuses?

I can only marvel at the incredible life that has evolved on our planet, and feel lucky to have seen my share of it.

The difficulties begin as soon as you compare an ape's mind to the mind of a human. You are now entering the realm of hominization, which is the process of becoming human. Much effort is put into understanding the cognitive abilities of early hominins and which traits set us apart from our primate ancestors.

Hominization is naturally biased toward modern humans and places them at the top of a pyramid. And as far as pure cognitive abilities—reasoning, problem-solving, abstract thinking—we might just belong there. Students of hominization think that in a world full of exceptional creatures, these capabilities make us unique. For them, it's all about the intellect.

Even gorillas and chimps that have been taught sign language or to use computers are no match for us on that level. They have no concept of how the computers work.

But animals can express love, empathy, and even show respect.

Gorillas can detect odors that belie the presence of unfamiliar apes. They can also smell the reproductive status of females. The vision of monkeys is second only to raptors like hawks and eagles, and they can hear not only the low range of sound that the humans can listen to but also sounds in the higher ultrasonic range.

Is it possible with all these additional abilities that they perceive a world that is fuller and more complex? Just how incredible must life appear when experienced by creatures with senses so much more developed than ours?

And who would not want to see the world through their eyes? Oh, to be an ape for a day!

It may have been sheer luck that our ancestors ended up in an environment that, over time, encouraged complex, abstract thought. Somewhere along the way—through the millennia—that route led to us pondering our own existence.

I have an overactive mind. As soon as I awake, I am up for the day. Once my mind begins running, it rarely lets me go back to sleep. And it takes a concerted effort to pull it away from subjects — however counterproductive — that it has taken a liking to.

So, the idea of being a creature with a bit less self-awareness and more sensory awareness is appealing to me.

Many primates pass the red dot test when facing a mirror, but they do not then use the mirror to improve their appearance, as humans do.

Unlike us, they also do not become self-conscious when they realize it is their own appearance being reflected.

But with humans, before their second year, most infants that are placed in front of a mirror will coo and smile with delight. When they become a little older, a radically different behavior arises. They show embarrassment and turn away or hide their face behind their hands.

This is because the next step in human self-awareness is not only recognizing yourself but seeing how others perceive you.

When Biami tribesmen in Papua New Guinea were first shown mirrors or images of themselves, they were paralyzed with fear, covering their mouths or hiding their heads the way a three-year-old might.

Suddenly discovering how others see you can be a scary thing.

I have never heard of this behavior in apes, although it is clear there is an awareness at work in their minds.

And maybe that is what I enjoyed about my time with the apes: They were not really interested in how I saw them.

In this novel, I have tried not to focus too much on the accomplishments that apes completed in captivity. My stories are all from the wild and were written by a layman, not a scientist or conservationist. And much of these stories took place in the last century before a lot of the current research was even conceptualized.

I also feel that saying an ape "has the equivalent intelligence of a third-grader" is demeaning. Don't get me wrong, I have a third grader right now, and she is clever.

Yet apes are so much more than slightly diminished versions of ourselves.

Thru natural selection, the mutations and genetic drift that occurred over their evolutionary history have fine-tuned them to be best suited for their environment.

In my eyes, they are perfect.

And I hope that through some of these stories, you see them as the magical, loving, intelligent and peaceful animals that I have come to know.

In the Virungas with a young
mountain gorilla. 1993.

Panamanian rainforest, as seen from Canopy Tower. 2000.

Safeguarding their Future

Conservation
(2019)

I was born in 1964, two years before Dian Fossey began her work with the mountain gorillas. It would be a decade before I started learning about her efforts, and during my early teens helping endangered species seemed like fun.

Little did I realize at the time that helping animals thrive in the wild meant not just preserving their habitat but preventing them from being killed by humans.

I remember reading a quote by Fossey and not realizing she was talking about an ongoing war.

"Conservation of any endangered species must begin with stringent efforts to protect its natural habitat by the enforcement of rigid legislation against human encroachment into parks and other game sanctuaries."

Although Fossey was the first to conduct a long-term study of the apes, she also spent much of her time destroying snares and scaring off poachers. She clearly believed that without her anti-poaching efforts, there would be no mountain gorillas left to study at all.

But she had arrived ready to fight.

When discussing with Dr. Leakey her preparations to depart from America, he had jokingly suggested she have her appendix taken out—just to be safe—because if it ruptured there, she wouldn't have access to a good hospital.

Weeks before she got on the plane to East Africa, she had it removed.

After that, she never looked back.

In 1978 she recorded that someone had ransacked Carl Akeley's tomb and left his remains scattered about the meadow. She knew it was the local witch doctors, or *umushitsi*, who sometimes added human bones to their sumu pouches, which are used as amulets for good or evil.

Fossey reburied what was left of Akeley's remains and spent considerable effort calming her staff, who suspected the bones had been stolen to make bad magic against her.

And they probably weren't wrong. Fossey had become the number one enemy for poachers in the area, and as the game at the base of the Virungas began to be hunted out, the poachers slowly moved higher into the volcanic mountains.

Into the territory of the mountain gorillas.

To prepare themselves, the poachers requested talismans from the witch doctors to help them fight the mad American woman, who seemed to care only about the gorillas.

These were dangerous times in Africa, and many locals didn't appreciate the efforts of conservationists who seemed to only care about the animals and not the plight of the people.

And Fossey pushed the limits of conservation with highly contested methods, including the kidnapping and torture of suspected poachers.

Two years later, in 1980, Joy Adamson was murdered in Kenya. Joy had become well-known after the release of *Born Free*, and her death made international news.

In 1985, Fossey was discovered murdered in her cabin at the Karisoke Research Center, located in the peaceful meadow between Mount Karisimbi and Mount Bisoke.

She is buried there, next to her gorilla friend, Digit, in a cemetery she created for gorillas killed by poachers - likely the same people who killed her.

And then in 1989, George Adamson died after being shot by poachers.

And there were plenty of others — far too many — whom I have not covered in this book, scientists and conservationists who gave their lives in the hopes that one day the animals they loved could survive in the wild without the threat of extinction looming over them.

In 1990 — when I was on my way to Sumatra, where I would eventually get lost and become surrounded by orangutans — my friend Penelope Bodry-Sanders was on her way to Zaire to locate Carl Akeley's grave.

Shortly before her arrival, someone had ransacked the grave, leaving his bones exposed in an open pit.

Had the witch doctors returned? Or had it been looters?

Nobody knew. Most of the locals had long forgotten Akeley, who had died over seventy years earlier.

And maybe that's how Akeley would have wanted it. He knew very well what happened to a gorilla's body when it died. Apes do not bury their dead in some hidden spot, like the mythical elephant graveyard that eluded explorers for years.

Their bodies naturally decompose where they drop after the scavengers have their say.

Maybe the plundering of his bones was the final price Akeley had to pay for the killing he had done.

Yet, those who knew of his legacy thought he deserved more respect.

The park rangers had reburied the bones, but Bodry-Sanders took extra measures to make sure Akeley wasn't disturbed again. She hired a string of porters to lug heavy bags of cement up the mountain and fortified and rebuilt his gravesite before leaving.

Doctor Livingstone took no chances with what would happen with his body and left explicit instructions for his servants. Upon his death, they cut out his heart and buried it under a great baobab tree — this way, a part of the great explorer would always remain in Africa.

Then they mummified his body with salt, wrapped it in cloth, and carried it by hand back to the coast, a journey of more than a thousand miles that took months. From Zanzibar, Livingstone's remains were shipped back to England, where he was laid to rest in the nave of Westminster Abbey.

And why would these two men go through such an ordeal?

It is because even when Livingstone was old and maybe a little senile, he still had hope.

He wanted to discover the source of the White Nile. And in his wanderings, he explored much of the interior of the African continent. He followed the Zambezi north and west, into Angola and then to the Atlantic. And on his return journey, he became the first European to cross the entire African continent when he exited the mighty river's mouth and entered the Indian Ocean.

He loved Africa, and he always hoped to discover more of it.

He always yearned for what was around the next bend in the river.

Maybe that's why his servants were so loyal — they understood his love of Africa, their homeland.

And that is a view shared by many of the explorers and conservationists who set foot on that continent: There's something magical about Africa, its people, and the wild animals.

Something that should be preserved.

In this book, I have touched upon some of the last century's scientific expeditions to Africa, Asia and the Amazon, where un-mapped places were sought, and animals were collected for museum exhibits.

I've always been fascinated by these explorations. Still, I recognize that most of the African locations "explored" by Burton,

Speke or Livingstone were already inhabited, or known, by local people

During some of these expeditions, the locals were at times treated with less respect than the exotic animals they searched for.

And in colonial times, when foreigners encountered indigenous people, they often enslaved them, exposed them to diseases, and just took their lands.

People like Theodore Roosevelt and Carl Akeley took part in these hunts, and although I understand their reasons, a hundred and fifty years later, I wish they'd found another way.

Roosevelt went on to set aside 150 million acres of the United States as national forest. In 1905 he helped create the present-day United States Forest Service and National Park Service. Soon after, he established fifty-one Federal Bird Reserves that would later become today's National Wildlife Refuges.

Perhaps it was guilt over the killing he'd done that drove him, or he might have simply wanted to return the land to the way he'd first experienced it. Either way, his conservation legacy is still alive today.

And we all owe our gratitude to the park rangers and other conservationists who struggle daily to protect animals from humans.

If you want to get involved with apes and conserving their habitats, I've got a few recommendations: The Jane Goodall Institute (www.janegoodall.org) and the Dian Fossey Gorilla Fund International (www.gorillafund.org) are each active in conserving ape habitats. Both websites are also full of information about ongoing projects.

You will also want to check out the work of The Explorers Club (www.explorers.org) and the American Museum of Natural History (www.amnh.org). Both organizations offer grants to scientists and conservationists conducting field research.

On a personal level, I've found myself lost or in desperate straits in some remote corner of the world, on more than one occasion. In many of these instances, the only reason I made it out was that an indigenous person came to my rescue.

A local. Someone who knew the forest, jungle or savannah.

I owe these caretakers of the natural world a great debt.

It has been encouraging to see that over the last fifty years, indigenous people and local communities have become central to many conservation movements. Although the real breakthroughs only began when we started listening to them instead of telling them how to manage the land.

These days, there is a strong effort to decolonize conservation, and the rogue actions of people like Dian Fossey are very much frowned upon. Today's efforts place indigenous people in the lead; they depend on these ecosystems for their very existence, and by contributing their traditional knowledge with attempts to protect the land, they have made a difference.

But global deforestation and climate change have rapidly created problems that they cannot solve alone.

The Earth's 6th major extinction event — otherwise known as the Holocene or Anthropocene extinction — is well underway. Habitat loss, greenhouse gas emissions, human population growth and increasing per capita consumption are the primary drivers of this decline. Current extinction rates are estimated at 100 to 1,000 times higher than normal; and are being propelled by the degradation and destruction of coral reefs, rainforests, and other habitats.

Our planet's loss of wildlife is staggering. In the last fifty years, we have lost two-thirds of all the mammals, birds, fish and reptiles. Amphibian populations worldwide are crashing, as are the numbers of bats and insects. Last year alone, the United States lost 44% of its bees and 86% of its Monarch butterflies.

We need to reconsider our eating habits and the use of harmful pesticides. Humans account for about 36 percent of the biomass of all mammals, domesticated livestock — mostly cows and pigs — account for 60 percent, and wild mammals for only 4 percent. The

228

number of domestic chickens actually outnumbers all the wild birds combined!

Even today, we have only a poor understanding of how most ecosystems work. Climate change and our overexploitation of the natural world put us at closer and more frequent exposure to germs and bacteria that might prove harmful to humans. The COVID-19 epidemic is one case in point because genetic analysis suggests that it originated in wild animal populations and then jumped to humans.

The Centers for Disease Control and Prevention state on their website that, "Scientists estimate 3 out of every 4 new or emerging infectious diseases in people come from animals."

Proceeding cautiously with the future in mind is the only real option; otherwise, zoonotic diseases may become much more frequent.

Luckily, there are some very noble attempts to change our planet for the better. The Thirty by Thirty movement is an initiative to protect thirty percent of the land and water in the United States by 2030. Currently, only twelve percent of America is protected from development.

The Global Deal for Nature (www.globaldealfornature.org) would take that a step further by creating a separate plan for each of the world's 846 terrestrial ecoregions. This initiative would be a companion to the Paris Climate Agreement, with the goal of protecting half of the terrestrial realm. Key objectives include promoting increased habitat protection and restoration, national and regional conservation strategies, and the empowerment of indigenous peoples to protect their sovereign lands.

In both plans, once the lands were protected, some would be accessible for outdoor recreation, but any wholesale degradation or destruction of these habitats would be restricted, including oil and gas development.

Please take the time to examine some of these initiatives and think about what you might do personally. It will take a global effort, but together we can reverse the current species extinction crisis and ensure the long-term health of our planet.

In closing, I have one positive takeaway that I will leave you with. It's not much when set against the challenges conservationists face today, but it is my wish that it brings you a little hope. Because hope is not just a dream—hope is laying out the plans to get something done.

And if we all work together, I believe we can change this world and help sustain the environments not only where primates live but for all wild animals.

The study of animal intelligence is ever-expanding, with neuroscientists, psychologists, anthropologists, and philosophers joining zoologists in unraveling the nature of animal cognition, emotion and sentience.

But if we don't prevent their habitats from being developed, many primates may not be around for much longer. It is my wish that by reading my stories, you might appreciate primates more and see the importance of saving their environment.

At least, I hope so.

In a recent census conducted in the Virunga Volcanoes, they counted a minimum of 604 individuals. When combined with the known individuals in Uganda's Bwindi Impenetrable National park—about 400 individuals—that pushes the number of wild mountain gorillas living in the wild to over 1,000.

Hopefully, Oscar is still one of them.

Impala. Serengeti plain, Tanzania. 1998.

Conclusion

Bare Attention
(2020)

What I gathered from my experiences with primates was that they gave me hope. It may be that by spending enough time with horses, or dogs, or any other animal, I might eventually know them well enough that I might have the same experience.

Yet, it's so much easier with primates because we recognize many of their facial expressions and hand gestures. They are familiar to us like no other animal, with mental states in which they exhibit emotions, desire and understanding. It's no wonder we are prone to anthropomorphize apes when we discuss them.

I have never had an issue with attributing a Theory of Mind to the greater apes. Most theory of mind experiments on animals are variations of cognition tests done on children and infants.

It's a very controversial topic, and the only consensus seems to be that consciousness does not exist in animals in the same way it exists in humans. But just because apes are not self-aware on the same level as humans (at least from what we can tell) doesn't mean they lack conscious minds.

Without verbal language, you would not have a running dialogue in your brain, but you would still have a stream of consciousness. And much of the exciting science done today demonstrates that animals think in languages that can be quite complex even without words.

A scent trail is a language, as is a bird call. A slime trail of a snail also communicates information to other snails and other animals. Facial expressions are certainly a language if you know how to interpret them. These discoveries give me hope that someday we will stop killing wild animals, maybe understand them a little better, and learn how to live with them without feeling the need to exert our dominance over them.

Merriam-Webster's definition of hope is "to want something to happen or be true."

And the more we study hope, the more we realize it is more than just a desire for a specific outcome. It differs from optimism, too, in that optimism is about anticipating the best possible result, whereas hope often requires one to create goals and the strategies to reach them.

Early African explorers were filled with hope, but they were also obsessed with the unknown. When it came to Africa, they had little choice. Explorers and their cartographers had little information to go by. In most cases, they simply left vast parts of their maps black and labeled it *terra incognita* – or unknown land.

Mighty rivers like the Niger, the Zambezi and the Nile had been known for centuries, but no one knew their headwaters' locations. And fabled desert kingdoms like Harar, Meroë, and Timbuktu inspired men to brave the Sahara Desert and explore it to learn what was truly there.

What spurred them on was a burning curiosity, along with a desperate dream to unravel the unknown.

They simply had to know more—had to prove that something existed.

In the same way, conservationists were drawn to the apes.

Fossey, Goodall, and Galdikas, who have studied and protected these primates, did so because, in some ways, they saw primates — especially the great apes — as windows into our own souls.

234

In so many ways, the great apes resemble us with minds that embrace problem-solving and individual personalities. They exhibit emotions like anger, sadness, contentment and despair, and, perhaps most importantly, curiosity. After all, if you watch a great ape for any amount of time, the first thing you'll notice is their intense curiosity.

In many ways, it is curiosity that made us what we are. Curiosity makes us independent and forces us to develop skillsets for survival. In fact, studies have shown that adults who exhibit high curiosity live longer lives.

In his recent book, *The Explorers*, Martin Dugard lists seven common traits possessed by legendary explorers: passion, courage, curiosity, hope, independence, self-discipline, and perseverance. While pondering this list, I realized these were also traits needed to be a good conservationist.

Both explorers and conservationists must live in the moment and be mindful of an environment that is often different and more dangerous than the one they were raised in. They make sacrifices too, often subjecting themselves to tropical diseases, human conflicts, and environmental dangers, and in some cases, forfeiting their lives.

They must be fiercely independent, but this part might come easy because many are driven by goals that push them beyond what is expected of most people with ordinary lives. Most explorers and conservationists view their work as being larger than their individual lives.

And maybe that's why they didn't let the harsh African sun, or the numerous tropical maladies, stop them.

Whenever I returned from a trip to Africa, it always irked me a little when people asked me if I had fun. Traveling in Africa was many things — exciting, dangerous, exhausting — and to call it fun made it sound too easy.

I had to avoid dengue fever, malaria, yellow fever, hepatitis, cholera, dysentery and giardia — not always successfully. I was attacked by red ants, leeches, centipedes, mosquitos, spiders and scorpions, had run-ins with spitting cobras, vipers and black mambas. I won't even get into my troubles with elephants, rhinos and hippos—or one very mean honey badger.

And I've had encounters with man as well, from border guards who sought bribes to thieves and bandits who held me up at knife- or gun-point.

Still, my troubles are only a shadow of what Speke and Burton went through in the mid-1800s. On their first journey to Africa, Speke barely escaped with his wrists tied and eleven spear wounds. Burton fled down a beach with a spear sticking through his head. It had passed through his mouth, in one check and out the other, knocking out two molars in the process.

In comparison, I got off easy.

Earlier on, I mentioned how psilocybin had the ability to knock one out of their default mode network. And how in that state, our minds may simplify things. Thoughts about the past or future dissipate, and as the "I" fades away, many may feel they are watching themselves from a distance, from a 3rd person perspective. Yet, they also felt intimately connected to life around them.

When I first mentioned this effect, I thought I might better understand an ape's mind if I made my own a bit less self-aware. But the reality is, even if I slipped out of my default network after taking psilocybin, I was still under the influence of a drug—and that can confuse things.

But I had felt I was on to something there. We spend much of our time filled with anxiety, unable to stay grounded in the present moment. It's not just me. All humans ponder the past, questioning their decisions, and anticipating the future. We have busy minds, and they don't like to be idle.

Maybe that is why the idea of a primitive version of us living in the Garden of Eden is so appealing to me. To go back to that state of innocence, existing in the moment, while conscious but not as self-aware.

To be part of nature, not just an observer of nature.

After we became self-aware, there was no going back. We may blame it on a religious perspective that states we were kicked out of the Garden, but the truth is we ejected ourselves. Apparently, once you eat the fruit from the tree that contains the "knowledge of good and evil"—or in our case, develop the default mode network—you enter the world of symbolization, metaphor, and language. And from that point on, it's a challenge to stay in the moment.

And that's where the Garden exists—in the moment.

But it is more challenging than it sounds to stay in the moment because everything is impermanent. The breath comes in and out, thoughts arise and vanish, sensations come into being and pass. All these phenomena are in constant flux. In fact, all the elements of body and mind exist for only an instant before vanishing—a process that happens continuously.

There are many ways we can train our minds to slip out of the default mode network. Meditation, prayer, high-adrenaline sports and even fear can be effective for short periods of time. But none achieved what I sought after.

What I was looking for turned out to be a quality of mind called bare attention. This concept involves one observing things as they are without choosing or comparing. It requires you to withhold the evaluation of what is happening in the moment or the formation of any expectations.

In his book, *The Experience of Insight*, Joseph Goldstein describes "bare attention" as the basis and foundation of spiritual discovery. He describes the experience as "cultivating a choiceless and non-interfering awareness." Bare attention keeps us awake and focused on the here and now, experiencing fully what is currently happening.

It reminded me of the state of mind I often found myself in when observing animals or nature; when the magic of a place enchanted me so much that I just wanted to take it all in and become a part of it. Many of those encounters have stayed with me throughout my life—quite vividly—and to revisit them, I simply open the door in my mind.

One, in particular, was the quietness of Panama's Chagres River after I had screamed in unison with the howlers at a thunderstorm overhead.

During that event, my mind was void of thought, filled only with the need to release.

I was the rain, the heat, the insects.

I was the crash of the lightning and the booming thunder.

I was a howl.

But in my memory, my voice is silent. Like I never uttered a sound.

Afterward, I felt white-washed in a sense. This was no ordinary experience for me. It had been no barbaric yawp — no tribute to Whitman. This was a primal experience, and it left me feeling somewhat like a ghost.

When I finally sat in the boat on the turgid river, I was still in a funk where my mind was clear of thought. There was no chatter in my brain.

Instead, I recollected images of moving through the wet, hot jungle. Watching the storm. Shouting at it until I was hoarse. Watching it pass. Impelled only by the most primitive of instincts. Defiantly surviving.

And while the guide and boat operator prepared for our departure, I finally let other impressions into my mind – the exotic bird calls, the countless insects, creaking trees along the shore, a frog croaking, and the dark-bellied clouds racing by overhead.

Even today, that memory is so overwhelming that I sway with it as the strong breeze flowing up the river pushes me. I see the flooded shore, looking up to its neck in water. I feel the cleanness of the air that comes after a heavy storm has passed through.

I observe it all with a quiet mind, and for a brief time, I am in the Garden again.

Why do I recall this so vividly? Did I take a bare attention "snapshot" of that moment on the river? Or was it my interaction with the howlers that provokes such a vivid recollection?

All I know is that primates have been involved in most of the profound nature experiences I have ever had. They quieted my mind, and I liked myself better when I was around them. These experiences made me want to return to the wild, to commune with the apes again, to immerse myself further into nature and strive to become one with it.

Over the years I learned a lot about primates, but in the end, I learned more about myself. My fifty-year obsession with apes has left me with a definite case of Pithecophilia that seems unlikely to abate, and I'm okay with that.

I recall my old black-and-white photo of the Lone Male, and I can imagine I see a slight smile on his face, but I know that's just me anthropomorphizing.

Yet, in my mind, the apes I encountered are still watching me, waiting to see if I can truly calm my anxious psyche.

Because only then can I be a member of the tribe again, and with that comes readmittance to the Garden.

Pithecophilia

Glossary

Many of these terms have complex definitions. I have modified their meaning to correlate with how I used the words in this novel.

Allomothering – When someone other than the genetic mother or genetic father takes part in the care or bringing up of an infant. This behavior is widespread among mammals and birds.

Animal conservation – The protection and preservation of animals and the habitats they require.

Anthropomorphize – Attributing human behavior or emotions to the actions of animals.

Bare Attention – The clear and single-minded awareness of what happens to us and in us at the moment of perception.

Cognitive abilities – Mental capabilities for the performance of higher mental processes, reasoning through intelligence and remembering.

Consciousness – The state of being awake and aware of one's surroundings.

Default Mode Network – A large-scale brain network that is active when an individual is thinking about themselves, remembering the past, or planning the future.

Genus – A category of biological classification which is above the species and below the family level. The genus is also the first half of a Linnean species name. For example, "*Homo*" is the genus for *Homo sapiens*.

Hominization – The development of human characteristics through evolution. It is these characteristics that distinguish hominins from their primate ancestors.

Inner dialogue – The running narrative in one's head that combines conscious thoughts with subconscious beliefs and biases. In humans, this is composed of words, created when we think but don't vocalize.

Matriarchal and Patriarchal – Social organizations in which a female (matriarchal) or a male (patriarchal) is the head.

Mirror Test – A measure of self-awareness that looks at what animals do when confronted with their mirror image and whether they can recognize their own reflection.

Mutualism – A relationship between two organisms in which both benefit. This occurs when two organisms live symbiotically.

Sapience – The ability to consciously contemplate thinking with access to memories. It is often defined as wisdom or judgment.

Self-awareness – The state of being aware of one's existence, personality and nature. The ability to conceive of oneself as separate from the environment.

Sentience – The capacity to feel, perceive, or experience subjectively. Sentient animals can experience pleasure and are motivated to seek it.

Stream of Consciousness – A continuous unedited chronological sequence of thoughts and inner reactions flowing through the mind.

Theory of Mind – The ability to attribute mental states like desires, emotions, and knowledge to oneself and others and grasp that others have beliefs and desires different from one's own.

A few Explorers and Scientists

Charles Darwin 1809 - 1882

Dr. David Livingstone 1813 - 1873

Richard Francis Burton 1821 - 1890

Alfred Russel Wallace 1823 - 1913

John Hanning Speke 1827 - 1864

Paul Du Chaillu 1831 - 1903

Henry Morton Stanley 1841 – 1904

Explorers Club members & medalists

(mentioned in this book)

Theodore Roosevelt (HON 1915) 1858 - 1919

Carl Akeley (AcNR 1912) 1864 - 1926

Roy Chapman Andrews (HON 1908) 1884 - 1960

Marlin Perkins (AcNR '51) 1905 - 1986

Neil Armstrong (MED '71) 1930 - 2012

Jim Fowler (MED '66) 1930 - 2019

Don Walsh (MED '61)

Dian Fossey (FNR '82) 1932 - 1985

George Schaller (MED '77)

Jane Morris Goodall (MED '93)

Robert Ballad (MED '78)

Donald Johansson (MED '76)

Alfred McLaren (MED '71)

Penelope Bodry-Sanders (FN '89)

Kiboko with his tribe.

Robert Louis DeMayo is a native of Hollis, N.H., but has lived in many corners of the planet. He took up writing at the age of twenty when he left his job as a biomedical engineer to explore the world. His extensive journaling during his travels inspired four of his novels and far-reaching work for the travel section of *The Telegraph*, out of Nashua, NH, as well as the *Hollis Times*. He is a member of The Explorers Club and chair of its Southwest Chapter.

His undying hunger for exploration led to a job marketing for Eos Study Tours, a company that served as a travel office for six non-profit organizations and offered dives to the *Titanic* and the *Bismarck*, Antarctic voyages, African safaris and archaeological tours throughout the world.

For several years after that, Robert worked as a tour guide in Alaska and the Yukon during the summers and as a jeep guide in Arizona during the winter. He was made general manager of the jeep tour company but eventually left the guiding world to write full time.

DeMayo is the author of seven novels: "The Making of Theodore Roosevelt," a fictionalized account of Roosevelt´s first acquaintance with wilderness living; "The Light Behind Blue Circles," a mystery thriller set in Africa; "The Wayward Traveler," a semi-autobiographical story following a young traveler on his adventures abroad; "Pledge to the Wind, The Legend of Everett Ruess," a fictionalized account of the life and times of the young solo traveler of the American West; "The Road to Sedona," the story of a young family that heads up to Alaska to find work in the wake of 9/11; and recently, "The Sirens of Oak Creek," a historical mystery of Oak Creek Canyon, Arizona spanning twelve centuries. Collectively, his novels have won eight national awards.

Currently, he resides in Sedona, AZ, with his wife Diana and three daughters: Tavish Lee, Saydrin Scout, and Martika Louise.

Pithecophilia

Acknowledgments

I owe a great debt of thanks to the various Explorers Club members that helped me with this book, notably Ed Sobey and Jut Wynne, Ph.D., who offered advice on the Conservation section. Lacey Flint, at the Club HQ in NYC, was very helpful in sorting out past members and their contributions to the club. Scott Trageser, David Dolan and Nancy Nenow also provided advice and contacts for research. And I want to extend a huge thank you to Penelope Bodry-Sanders, who sponsored me to get into TEC and first introduced me to Carl Akeley's Hall of African Mammals at AMNH.

Additionally, I would like to thank the people that helped me craft this story: Nina Rehfeld edited the novel, and after, Jut Wynne, Ph.D., reviewed the entire story to make sure I didn't drift too far from scientific truth.

Andrew Holman did an outstanding job taking a drawing by Tom Fish and turning it into a cover. Friends who read early drafts and helped me define concepts include Mark Patton, Jeff Gobel, Bob Brill, Martin Gray and Alexis Mendez.

Pithecophilia

Former Disney illustrator, Tom Fish, went above and beyond for me on this project, completing not just the cover image but the incredible drawings at the start of each chapter in Book One. Not only did he draw the primates featured in each story, but he matched their sex, age, and, when possible, their nature as depicted in the story.

Thanks also to Todd Nielsen, my former employer at Eos Study Tours, who read a few sections and offered comments, and Ian Tattersall, who I dined with at an Explorers Club annual dinner in 2001. His book on evolution and human uniqueness, *Becoming Human*, greatly influenced me and this work.

I would also like to shout out to my former traveling companions, some like Vendu and Franco, I never saw again. But others have kept in touch regularly. Perhaps our time together with apes created an "in my tribe for life" bond. James Shawcross was the young man I journeyed with when visiting the gorillas. Almost thirty years later, we still talk about it. He continued to travel Africa, too, and today is a Fellow of the Royal Geographic Society.

Thank you to my writing group members, particularly Kim Boykin and Claire Obermarck, for offering insightful criticism and praise for early drafts.

And last but not least, my wife, Diana, and three girls, Tavish, Saydrin and Martika, who all listened to these stories over the years—and then again while I worked on this novel. As I've grown older, it seems many past events simply become anecdotes that fade with time. If it wasn't for the excited sparkle in the eyes of my daughters when I talked of being surrounded by orangutans or charged by a mountain gorilla, I might have just shelved them. So, thank you, girls, for all your encouragement.

Robert Louis DeMayo

Also by **Robert Louis DeMayo**

"This book explores an aspect of Theodore Roosevelt's life that is not usually addressed when it comes to information regarding this president. Although this is a fictionalized story, DeMayo perfectly presents the essence of a young Roosevelt. The story is based on local recollections of Roosevelt's visits to the wilds of Maine, where he learned the ways of the woods. DeMayo seamlessly captures the local vernacular and paints an accurate picture of the time in which the story is set. The story is an enjoyable read that is appropriate for young adults as well as adults."
–Kathleen Kallfelz

THE MAKING OF THEODORE ROOSEVELT

This a fictionalized account of a true story – the tale of how two rough Maine woodsmen took a young Theodore Roosevelt under their wing in 1878 and introduced him to the beautiful but unforgiving woodlands of the Northeast. Under their guidance, the frail but strong-willed New Yorker becomes a worthy outdoorsman. This experience significantly shaped the world view of the man poised to become the 26th President of the United States thirteen years later.

Historical Fiction.
Wayward Publishing.
Available in print, eBook
& audiobook.

Also by **Robert Louis DeMayo**

"Reading this exquisitely written work should inspire anyone to want to live a simpler life with endearing respect for nature. It is almost unfathomable that someone as young as Everett Ruess could have such a profound look at society and the way it can strangle the purity and life out of so many. Robert Louis DeMayo captures both the country's beauty and an individual's quest for beauty in its simplest form. This book makes one want to pack up and visit the glorious beauty of the southwest similarly, to try to even remotely see life through the unadulterated eyes of a young man who dared to live life on his own terms."

–Tim Glover

PLEDGE TO THE WIND, THE LEGEND OF EVERETT RUESS

Eighty years ago, a young man disappeared in the Utah wilderness. An extensive search followed, but all they turned up was his last camp and a couple of burros. Numerous historical books have been published that attempt to prove what happened to Everett, but his fate remains one of the biggest mysteries of the southwest. Pledge to the Wind, the Legend of Everett Ruess follows the adventures of Everett Ruess from his appearance in the southwest in 1931 when he was barely seventeen, until his disappearance in 1934, shortly before he turned 21. This historical fiction novel focuses more on how he lived from day to day, the adventures he experienced, and the language he used to express them. Upon reading it, Brian Ruess wrote, "In this work of fiction ... I saw Everett for the first time, as he might actually have been."

Historical Fiction.
Wayward Publishing.
Available in print, eBook
& audiobook.

Also by **Robert Louis DeMayo**

"I enjoyed this book immensely. It is a way to see the world from the safety of your home and yet feel like you are experiencing the thrills, adventures, fears and exhilaration along with the main character, Louis. This book is so well-written that I didn't want to put it down as I followed Louis's adventures around the world. He met every type of person...from the dangerous to the glorious and everything in between. His descriptions of animal encounters left me breathless and envious for the same experiences. If you have any interest in traveling and a general guideline for that and for life, you should read this book! I was so inspired, I applied for my passport...although I doubt I would ever be as willing to jump into adventure as Louis did."

–Heidi Benson

THE WAYWARD TRAVELER

This memoir-based novel follows the adventures of Louis, a young American who, in 1985, is determined to travel the world. The story takes place in forty countries and spans ten years: from the deck of a felucca on the Nile to the scorched dunes of India's Thar Desert to the mighty Beni River in the Amazon Basin. Louis feels disenchantment with his former life and a yearning to understand the foreign lands he encounters on his travels. He's broke most of the time and spends considerable effort trying to get by. Along the way, he develops a list of Rules to help him get by, and yet, there´s a restlessness to his travels. He continues to wander into new countries, and through it, all his Rules save him.

Fiction.
Wayward Publishing.
Available in print or eBook.

Made in the USA
Middletown, DE
22 March 2021